CONNECTICUT

MADE

CONNECTICUT
MADE

Cynthia Parzych

Globe
Pequot

Guilford, Connecticut

Globe
Pequot

An imprint of Rowman & Littlefield

Distributed by NATIONAL BOOK NETWORK

Copyright © 2016 Rowman & Littlefield

Photos by Cynthia Parzych or courtesy of the establishments.

British Library Cataloguing in Publication Information Available

Library of Congress Cataloging-in-Publication Data available
ISBN (paperback) 978-1-4930-1268-8
ISBN (e-book) 978-1-4930-2696-8

∞™ The paper used in this publication meets the minimum requirements of American National Standard for Information Sciences—Permanence of Paper for Printed Library Materials, ANSI/NISO Z39.48-1992.

All the information in this guidebook is subject to change. We recommend you call ahead to obtain current information before traveling.

Contents

Introduction

Connecticut has an enormous history of invention, innovation, high-quality product and craftsmanship, manufacturing, and most of all an entrepreneurial spirit, considering it is such a small state. This all started from the very beginning of its settlement by the English. John Winthrop Jr., the son of the first governor of the Massachusetts Bay Colony and the man who obtained the charter for Connecticut in 1662 from the British government, had the foresight to encourage scientists and alchemists to come to the state and cheerlead the development of the iron industry, which thrives here today, by starting one of the first iron ore mines in the American colonies in nearby Massachusetts. Eventually, Connecticut's first iron ore mine was opened in Salisbury in 1734, and when Ethan Allen built the first blast furnace in Lakeville in 1762, Connecticut's armaments business had its start, quickly building a reputation as the best in the developing new nation. As a testament to its quality and reputation, Allen's foundry manufactured the guns mounted on the deck of Old Ironsides, more than 800 cannons used in the American Revolutionary War, and even the chain that spanned the Hudson River at West Point to help prevent an attack by British ships, keeping them from moving up the key river in the war.

There are many other industries with early historical roots in Connecticut, which continue today or which have been reinvented to produce new products based on their earlier origins and reputations. Connecticut's boat and submarine business based in Groton and New London, founded in 1899 and today a backbone of the state's economy, traces its existence to the very first submarine in the world, built from oak in Connecticut by David Bushnell of Old Saybrook. The first submarine was used to attack the British ship *HMS Eagle* in New York Harbor on September 6, 1776. Many of the people behind other businesses with early origins in the state have been innovators, developing products never seen before. In addition to defense manufacturing, paper, textiles, furniture, pewter, firearms, clocks, bicycles, aircraft engines, ship building, hardware, tools, die-making, typewriters, sewing machines, financial services, insurance, medical innovation and research, and publishing all have roots and origins in Connecticut. For instance, the first tissue paper was made here; the nation's oldest continuously published (to this day) newspaper, the *Hartford Courant,* still operates; Amelia Simmons published the first US cookbook, *American Cookery*, in Hartford in 1796; Noah Webster published the first dictionary in the United States in 1806; the first phone exchange in the country was set up in New Haven on January 28, 1878; the first pay phone was set up in Connecticut; and one of the first American banks opened in Hartford in 1792. Friction-ignited matches were invented by Thomas Sanford in Beacon Falls in 1834, the Mickey Mouse watch was first produced by the Waterbury Clock Company in 1933, Silly Putty was invented in New Haven by an engineer working at General Electric in 1940, and Mounds and Almond Joy candies were first produced by The Peter Paul Candy Manufacturing Company in 1946.

How does such a small state attract so many great businesses? Well, the size of the state may just be one of the clues to the answer to that question. When a company becomes successful, other businesses spring up in reaction to that company's needs or as a result of a demand for services by the company. There's a symbiotic quality to success. Perhaps the tight-knit community that Connecticut has always been is just a very good place for ideas to incubate, be launched, grow, and spread, and also for businesses to cooperate with each other, as the distances are never very far within Connecticut's borders and there's certainly power when news of success is spread by word-of-mouth. The state's location between two key American east coast metropolises—New York and Boston—may have contributed as well. Plenty of people running companies in Connecticut expand their business to reach beyond the state's borders. Additionally, the presence of an excellent in-state college and university system (Connecticut was the first state to pay for public school education in 1795) is yet another factor that contributes to business development and an entrepreneurial spirit. Educational institutions feed ideas and advice, offer education and training to business owners and workers, provide expertise and manpower, and even direct their own business to companies just starting out, expanding, or moving to the state because of the close links that form between business and educational institutions—an excellent reason to set up a new business in Connecticut.

Since the turn of the 21st century, there's been an explosion of new ideas for small businesses in Connecticut. Perhaps the difficult economy was the incentive for many creative people to build their own businesses. Many businesses, as you will discover in this book, were started by baby boomers who dreamed an idea that cooked in their heads for years. Those baby boomers then retired, or got downsized from a life-long job, and decided it was time to take the leap and start a business. Some entrepreneurs have taken their education, the skills they've learned in their careers or from life experience, and have reinvented themselves by starting a new business. There have also been many revivals of old businesses, lost crafts and arts, and of local products that have contributed to the start of new companies set up by entrepreneurs, both young and old. Connecticut boasts such businesses as tavern sign-making; old crafts such as sailor's valentines and knot working; handmade instruments, shoes, and denim items; small batch and/or old fashioned alcoholic and non-alcoholic beverages, food products once the domain of the farmer and his wife, and cheesemaking. Other businesses have been cooked up in basements or garages all over Connecticut. They may have begun as a hobby or just a challenge, as many of the small-batch breweries have, springing up because friends have asked to buy their homemade beer. Or because a group of friends in Hartford who had never sewn in their lives decided to make their own jeans, resulting in demand for those jeans, leading to the launch of an exciting new business, Hardenco. Other business owners have committed themselves to doing something to help save the environment, establishing their businesses in once abandoned factories, mills, post offices, and other forgotten spaces where they recycle found materials and turn these into new products, such as furniture, lighting fixtures, musical instruments, decorative art, or fuel.

Mark Twain gives a perfect description of today's Connecticut small-business owners who are reinventing themselves and the state of Connecticut. He described in *A Connecticut Yankee in King Arthur's Court*, first published in 1889, the kind of entrepreneurs that you'll read about in *Connecticut Made*:

"Why, I could make anything a body wanted—anything in the world, it didn't make any difference what; and if there wasn't any quick new-fangled way to make a thing, I could invent one—and do it as easy as rolling off a log."

That pretty much sums up what this creative bunch of Connecticut business owners, whose stories you will read about in this book, have done and continue to do. Let their stories encourage you to visit Connecticut to meet them and see what they produce in factories, workshops, and studios all over the Nutmeg State.

How to Use This Book

The text of this book has been organized to make planning a trip in Connecticut to visit the state's craftspeople, small manufacturers, farmers, food and beverage producers, and other small businesses that make and sell interesting innovative products, convenient and easy. The main text of the book contains about 150 profiles of businesses that open their doors to the public (many by appointment only) so that visitors can see how and where they work. Broken into 17 product categories, the profiles are organized in alphabetical order under their appropriate headings. The name of the business, street address, town/city, phone, website link, and hours of operation (or where to find the opening days and times) opens each entry. Each entry contains information about the owner(s) of the business and some background about how/why the business began, a little history of the business, some local history or connection to the town or city where the business is located, and information about the products sold and what makes them special or unusual. As part of the backmatter of the book, you'll find the listing of all the businesses organized alphabetically by the town or city in which they are located with all the information you'll need to locate them, and a brief summary of the products they offer to make it easy to plan a day or weekend trip through Connecticut.

When planning a trip, be sure to check the times of operation for these small businesses. Most owners run their businesses from, do their own manufacturing in, or have their studios in the same space from which they sell their products. They grow, nurture, create, and/or practice their crafts as well as sell them to the public often single-handedly, so they are busy people. Farm stands, tasting rooms, and shops where you can buy cheese, vegetables, fruit, wine, beer, meat, and other products, are generally just one aspect of running a busy working farm, for instance. So the owners of small local businesses often have to juggle their time to be creative with hours devoted to running the commercial side of their businesses, which often results in limited hours of being open to the public.

Many of the craftspeople and food producers not only run their shops and galleries, but also attend farmers' markets and craft and/or trade shows throughout the state every month, which can also mean a business might unexpectedly not be open on a day you may intend to visit. So, if you should decide to plan a trip, it is always important to call ahead to be sure the places you wish to visit will indeed be open on the day you take your trip.

Because of the seasonal nature of farms, cheesemakers, and wineries, it is particularly important to check their websites and call ahead to be certain they will be there to open the door when you visit. The handcrafted beer business in Connecticut is booming and ever changing as these exciting businesses are popping up all over the state, and expanding and growing. This is yet another category of Connecticut product where it is important to check directly with the company to be sure it will be open when you decide to visit, or that they haven't moved to new premises as their sales and production grow to accommodate demand.

Please take the plunge and plan a visit to Connecticut with the intention of seeing the work of some of its most interesting small businesses and, of course, to support their efforts by buying Connecticut. You'll be delighted and entertained tremendously by the innovation and creativity of the state's many small entrepreneurs, and if you engage with these business owners, you'll learn that it's the interesting characters who live in this state who make it a dynamic place to live, to do business, and to visit.

Beer

Back East Brewery, 1296A Blue Hills Ave., Bloomfield 06002; (860) 242-1793; backeastbrewing.com. Tastings offered Wed through Fri, 4 to 7 p.m.; Sat, noon to 4 p.m. Two cousins, Tony Karlowicz and Edward Fabrycki, Jr., both Connecticut natives with a huge interest in beer, combined their talents to open this craft brewery. A reunion of the cousins and a home-brewing experiment in one of their garages in Southington, planted the seeds for the launch of this business in July 2012. They produce four standard craft beers—Golden Ale (American in style; light in body), Back East Ale (amber in color and medium in style), Misty Mountain IPA, and Porter, but they also make specialty beers, including a couple of big beers that they call the Hammer of the Gods series, which really pack a punch. The brewery

offers a 40-minute tour and tasting at a cost of $3 per person every Saturday, with four tours beginning on the hour from noon to 3 p.m. You'll not forget the

Willimantic Brewing Co.'s beer sampler is generous in quantity (see p.13).

enthusiastic and friendly welcome you'll receive. They are excellent hosts and the beers are delicious. They'll convince you to take home a growler of your favorite.

Beer'd Brewing Co., American Velvet Factory, 22 Bayview Ave., Unit 15, Stonington 06355; (860) 857-1014; beerdbrewing.com; open Fri, 5 to 9 p.m.; Sat and Sun, 1 to 5 p.m. Aaren Simoncini is the beard behind Beer'd Brewing, which opened in Stonington's artsy Velvet Factory maze of businesses in 2012. Yes, it's his beard on the distinctive logo and he makes all the beer. In addition to classic styles, Simoncini and his partner, Precious Putnam, produce several experimental beers. Their philosophy is to keep it small and make it all by hand to bring back the old American tradition of beer production and, most importantly, to maintain high quality. They have a small selection of beers, usually five offered for tasting at the

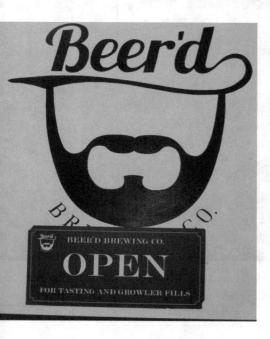

brewery, where you can also purchase growlers in two sizes (32 and 64 ounces) to take home. You might find any of these and then you might not; they often sell out their small batches of delicious beer by the end of the week because it is so popular with the locals. Whisker'd Wit is a particularly tasty brew, made in a Belgian dry style, with a hint of orange and spice. The beers certainly attract a crowd in the small but very attractive tasting area, but you'll find them a friendly and appreciative crowd when you visit, all standing together (there is limited seating), drinking beer, and sharing their views. The staff is knowledgeable and enthusiastic about the product they sell. It's a company you'll want to visit again when you are in the area.

Broad Brook Brewing Co., 2 North Rd., East Windsor 06088; (860) 623-1000; broadbrookbrewing.com. Open Wed, 3 to 7 p.m.; Thurs, 3 to 9 p.m.; Fri, 2 to 9 p.m.; Sat, noon to 7 p.m.; and Sun, noon to 5 p.m. This place is a little deceiving when you first approach, as it's located just off I-91 at the back of strip mall. But don't let that deter you! The staff is friendly, the tasting room is simple and comfortable, and the beer, made in small batches, is excellent. The owners—Ed Mance, Joe Alba, and master brewer Tom Rossing, were tired of drinking boring stuff, so they started to make their own full-bodied beers in 2010 in Rossing's garage. With encouragement from friends who tried their homemade brew, they opened their taproom a few years later. They named the company after the location of that garage where they made their first beer, and added a tobacco shed to their logo as a tribute to East Windsor's tobacco-producing history. In fact, the taproom bar is made from wood from a tobacco barn that blew down in a huge storm in 2011.

Broad Brook Brewing doesn't serve food in the tasting room, but you are encouraged to bring your own or have one of the local restaurants deliver—such a great idea that encourages patrons to drink a little more of the brewery's offerings. Broad Brook Ale (their signature beer), Oktoberfest Ale, and 7th Heaven appear to be their popular brews, but there are many others to taste, and each is very different in style and flavor. Season of the Witch is particularly interesting, as it's brewed with honey; but watch out, it's very strong. You can buy a flight of their many beers at a reasonable price, or, if you feel up to it, sample them all. And if you need to walk all that beer off, take their tour. You can also purchase growlers and there's lots of cool beer gear with their logo for sale. Free Wi-Fi is offered in the taproom.

Cottrell Brewing Company, 100 Mechanic St., Pawcatuck 06379; (860) 599-8213; cottrellbrewing.com. Open Fri, 3 to 6 p.m.; Sat, 1 to 6 p.m. Charlie Cottrell Buffum Jr. is the owner and brewmaster of this family-owned company, which he started with his wife, Anne, in 1997. In fact, together they rolled their first keg of Old Yankee Ale down Mechanic Street to their local bar, CC O'Brien's, a good spot to go and drink their beer on days when you can't taste it at the brewery. Buffum's love of British ale inspired him to make his own and that, in turn, became a new career and business for him. He gave the company the name of his ancestors, the Cottrells, who helped settle Westerly, Rhode Island, in 1666, just across the river. The Cottrells also built an international reputation in the late 19th and early 20th centuries as manufacturers of printing presses in Pawcatuck. Cottrell Brewing Company is located in an industrial park at the back of a warehouse and can be a little difficult to find, so consult their online map. There is no charge for tastings at their small tasting bar, which is set up among the beer-making equipment. They offer several of their four popular ales and different nano-brews weekly. It's a no-frills setup, so don't expect tables, chairs, and food! However, there are a few tables and chairs outside, where you can sit by the river on a warm day and take in the sun with a beer in hand. In addition, they sell a series of barrel-aged beers in bottles, as well as growlers or six-packs of their own beer on the premises.

Firefly Hollow Brewing Co., 139 Center St., Bristol 06010; (860) 845-8977; fireflyhollowbrewing.com. Open Thurs through Fri, 2 to 8 p.m.; Sat, noon to 8 p.m.; Sun, noon to 5 p.m. This business is housed in one of Bristol's many factories. Water Hammer, Ramshackle Golden Mild, Red Lantern, Toadstool Oat Stout, Photon Imperial Crimson, Lizard Breath IPA, and Nymph IPA are just a few of the more than 25 beers with crazy names that they sell. Usually three or four of those listed on the blackboard can be tasted and purchased in growlers at the brewery. The tasting room is no frills and industrial in style—lots of exposed wood and brick, high ceilings, and iron; the atmosphere is pleasant. Visitors are encouraged to bring in their own food. If you are lucky, you might arrive when the local food trucks do, so you can sample some local cooking washed down by beer made in Bristol. The place is crowded, which is a testament to the quality of the beer. The owners, Dana Bourque (the brewmaster) and Rich Loomis, have a great deal of experience in the many aspects of the world of beer (they used to own Brew & Wine Hobby, the Connecticut mecca for home wine and beer makers in East Hartford) and possess enormous enthusiasm for what they do. The beer really tastes like they know what they are doing.

Half Full Brewery, 43 Homestead Ave., Stamford 06902; (203) 658-3631; halfullbrewery.com. Open for tastings Fri, 4 to 7 p.m.; Sat and Sun, noon to 5 p.m. About four years after Conor Horrigan left a budding career in banking and dreamed up the idea of opening a brewery on a trip he took to see the world, it all came together and began to happen. He and a group of friends raised money, gathered together a small group of enthusiastic kindred spirits, and took a chance to begin making some very good beer. The doors of the brewery opened in 2012 in a renovated factory and they poured their first beer. Bright Ale, Pursuit IPA, and Toasted Amber are always available in their very cool tasting room, but you also might find a few seasonal brews such as Peach Wheat and Pumpkin Ale, made when those fruits are in season in Connecticut. On alternate Fridays they offer an open tap and food truck for a flat fee, or a half-price fee is charged to fill growlers with a pint thrown in at no charge with every growler filled. They also hold a pub run on Wednesdays, starting from their parking lot and heading to local places that sell their beer—a great bit of marketing for local sales of the beer. The taproom is spacious and open and feels more like a coffee house than a beer room, but it's friendly and appealing. Check the website regarding the Friday and Wednesday events, fees, and for tour times at the brewery.

New England Brewing Co., 175 Amity Rd., Woodbridge 06525; (203) 387-2222; newenglandbrewing.com. Open Wed through Fri, 3 to 7 p.m.; Sat, 11 a.m. to 4 p.m. Opening in 2003, this company was the first craft beer maker to put its beers in cans. Producing a long line of traditional lagers and ales and some more unusual brews sold on tap or in growlers only, they have made quite a splash in Connecticut because of their high-quality product and wise marketing. It's no secret that Nutmeggers love to drink beer out of a can! New England Brewing Co. has a small but very comfortable tasting room run by friendly people. It's always busy, and if you are already a fan, it's great to go in and taste something different on tap and bring home a growler of what appeals. It seems that many of the neighbors drop in to have a quick one and to buy a growler of fresh beer, so there's always a fun local crowd. They charge a fee for tasting their beers, so check the website for the price. Famous for their IPAs with crazy names, such as Sea Hag and G-Bot, they also offer Elm City Pilsner, which is a star and could be mistaken for a genuine German beer. On the final Friday of each month they have a party in the tasting room with a live band. Lots of fun, but be prepared for the crush in this small space.

Olde Burnside Brewing Company, 776 Tolland St., East Hartford 06108; (860) 528-2200; oldeburnsidebrewing.com. Open Sat, 1 to 4 p.m. There's Scottish ale being made by Robert McClellan in the center of East Hartford on the site of his family-run Burnside Ice Company, which his grandfather, Albert, started in 1933. Robert started the beer business in a garage on the ice company's property when he discovered a local man was producing excellent home-brew using the company's well water. The beer company, housed in a red brick building covered with hop vines, has been thriving since 2000. McClellan believes their success is due in large part to the high quality of pure water they use to make the beer. The water comes from their 400-foot well on the property that his father, Clifford, drilled in the 1960s to make ice. The excellent water, which, when analyzed, was found to be similar to the water used to make Bass Ale in Burton-on-Trent, England, and hops partially imported from England, make the selection of beers the company makes by hand in small batches the favorite of many Connecticut beer-heads. The flavor gets locked in when the beers are flash chilled on the premises right after they are made (remember they own an ice business!). This process also eliminates the need for pasteurization. Olde Burnside's main brew, Ten Penny Ale, can be found in almost any bar in the Connecticut River Valley on tap, and not just because it's local. It's malty and smoky with a slight hint of caramel—the same flavors that can be found when drinking many Scottish whiskies. It's a great beer to drink with food because of its high quality. Take the tour of the brewery any Saturday (you have to book in advance), followed by a tasting in the beer garden, which will set you back $10 per person.

Overshores Brewing Co., 250 East Bradley St., East Haven 06512; overshores .com. Check the website for opening times. Specializing in Belgian-style beer, which is the traditional accompaniment to that northern European country's popular dish of mussels cooked in beer with fries dipped in mayonnaise, Overshores Brewing Co. is right at home in East Haven. Owner Christian Amport probably did the right thing moving his operation a little closer to the coast and closer to Connecticut's once-abundant mussel supply, now slowly making a comeback. The company originally started in Killingworth in 2010 and then moved south to East Haven in 2013. Amport opened the doors to the new brewery in 2014, and brewmaster Brian Cox joined the operation. This is one of the few Connecticut breweries to date that makes Belgian-style beers, a favorite category of beer aficionados all over the world. The tasting room has charm, but it's pretty basic. The beers they offer (not all of them are their own) are an education in the style of beer made in Belgium. They quite cleverly present their own five beers against a backdrop of about a dozen other Belgian beers to which they compare theirs. They are all delicious. Take a free tour (offered when the bar is open). If you visit on a Friday night, they have live jazz and blues. They don't offer food, but do allow Amport's beer to inspire you to seek out a local joint to support the struggling mussel population. Also, be sure to ask for his beer wherever you choose to dine on the Connecticut shoreline.

Relic Brewing Co., 95 Whiting St., Plainville 06062; (860) 255-4252; relicbeer .com. Open Thurs and Fri, 4 to 7 p.m.; Sat noon to 4 p.m. Mark Sigman set up his boutique brewery in Plainville because the rents are cheap and he got the town council to approve the opening of the business without a hitch. The inspiration for the beer he makes comes from his travels in Europe. The industrial building his brewery is housed in is nondescript and a little hard to find because the sign is so small, but you'll get a warm and enthusiastic welcome when you do finally find them. The tasting area, decorated with art for sale by local artists, is very tiny and dark; only a half dozen people can fit in the space, which is the size of a small garage. There seems to be a constant flow of customers, however, not only to try free samples, but also to buy growlers. All the beer is made in very small seasonal batches as the size of the place dictates. Each type of beer has an interesting background story enthusiastically told by brewmaster Sigman, and every one of the beers is outstanding in quality. Try the Fortnight IPA, which is fruity and a little citrusy, or Houndstooth, a dark beer that is smooth with a bit of chocolate and coffee in the nose and flavor. If you find you like these brews, buy as much as you can because the word has gotten out that this stuff is great—many believe this is the best beer made in Connecticut—and you may not find it again. It appears that people line up more than an hour before Relic opens, with lawn chairs to sit on to conserve their energy for drinking this delicious stuff once they get inside the door. It's a no-frills experience with fantastic beer to enjoy (before each batch runs out)!

Shebeen Brewing Company, 1 Wolcott Rd., Wolcott 06716; (203) 514-2336; shebeenbrewing.com. Open Thurs through Fri, 5 to 9 p.m.; Sat, noon to 7 p.m.; Sun, noon to 5 p.m. Most Americans would call it a speakeasy and Nutmeggers would call it a dive, but the Irish call an illegal spot where alcohol is sold without a license a *shebeen* in Gaelic. Shebeen Brewing Company is completely legal, however, and opened its doors in 2013. Cofounder and head brewer, Rich Visco, was born in Northern Ireland and began to make beer at home in 1995. He and his partner drew up a business plan, which they put on hold until they saw the potential for their business in Connecticut 16 years later. They make very unusual beers indeed. Their Cucumber Wasabi, Cannoli (served in a glass with a sugar-coated rim with chocolate shavings sprinkled on the head!), Pumpkin Scotch Ale, Bacon Kona Stout, and Concord Grape Saison are just a few of their crazy ideas, which surprisingly are (mostly) pretty tasty. They also make some very good beers in a traditional style. The tasting room is no-frills with two rooms and a few tables and chairs and a great mural depicting an Irish street scene. There are picnic tables and rocking chairs outside. This has become a popular place, so expect a crowd. Check the website for the cost of tastings and don't forget to take the tour, the staff are enthusiastic and you'll learn a lot about making beer.

Thimble Island Brewing Company, 16 Business Park Dr., Branford 06405; (203) 208-2827; thimbleislandbrewery.com. The tasting room is open Thurs through Fri, 3 to 8 p.m.; Sat 11 a.m. to 8 p.m.; Sun noon to 5 p.m. Tours are available Sat at noon, 2, and 4 p.m., and Sun at 1 and 3 p.m. Justin Gargano and Mike Fawcett are two more Connecticut-born beer lovers who turned their hobby into a business. Starting out by making ale in their apartment, they eventually rented garage space, formed their business in 2010, and named it after the little cluster of islands just off Branford. They sold their first batch of beer, called American Ale, in 2012 to a local pub in Guilford. Drawing on a local product, they next made Coffee Stout with coffee beans from Willoughby's, a local coffee roaster. Coffee Stout, when they have it on tap, is one great reason to visit their tasting room, where you can always find their American Ale and a selection of other beers, all produced in small batches, including Windjammer Wheat Ale, and Ghost Island Double IPA, with names that are often reminders that their beer is made on the Connecticut coast. The staff is a friendly and generous group, the tastings are popular and lively, and the prices for the growlers (32 or 64 ounces) are reasonable.

Thomas Hooker Brewery, 16 Tobey Rd., Bloomfield 06002; (860) 242-3111; hookerbeer.com. Gift shop and growler-filling hours are Mon through Fri, 9 a.m. to 5 p.m.; Sat, noon to 5 p.m. Tastings are held the first and third Fri of every month from 5 to 8 p.m. When this business, named for Hartford founder Reverend Thomas Hooker, started in 2003, it was the beer-making arm of a bar/restaurant, the Trout Brook Brew Pub. Since 2006, it has had new owners, who moved it into new premises, expanded it, and grew the business into one of Connecticut's signature small brewers. It's reputation reaches well beyond the state as a quality producer of eight ales and five lagers in small batches and other specialty brews. Curt Cameron is the dynamic president, and his enthusiasm for the product is contagious. Arrive early for the weekend tastings, as there's usually a line to get in and to get a refill once you do enter the small tasting room. Hooker Blond is the signature beer, but they make special beers occasionally, like a chocolate beer using locally produced Munson's chocolate, and another one brewed from watermelon. For a charge of $10 on tasting days, take the tour, drink some beer, and get a pint glass to take home (part of the fee goes to a local charity). It's a fun way to spend a Saturday afternoon, when you can also take the tour and taste the whole range of beers. Buy a growler of the fresh beer produced that day to take home to remind you of where you've been—you just might need that reminder after an afternoon of tasting this excellent beer, as they are generous with the pouring in the tasting room.

Two Roads Brewing Co., 1700 Stratford Ave., Stratford 06615; (203) 335-2010; tworoadsbrewing.com. Open Tues through Sat, noon to 9 p.m.; Sun noon to 7 p.m. The four founders of this brewery started their lives in other businesses until they each came to crossroads in their careers and lives, and joined forces to start Two Roads. "Life always seems to offer up two ways to go," as they state on their website; there are always two roads. Taking that philosophy about life very seriously, and borrowing a line from the well-known Robert Frost poem for their company, they opened in 2012 and have applied that principle not only to their career choices, but also to the excellent beer they produce. Housed in the US Baird Building, a 100-year-old machine manufacturing factory, Two Roads offers classic beers from brewmaster Phil Markowski, but always with a different approach, or, as the poet wrote, "the road less traveled." This is perhaps most true of their seasonal beers, such as Road Jam, a wheat ale red in color and brewed with raspberries and lemongrass; Via Cordis, brewed with yeast from a very old monastic brewery in Belgium; Roadsmary's Baby, a pumpkin ale aged in rum barrels; and Conntucky Lightnin', a bourbon-like ale made from corn grits and aged in bourbon barrels. There are crazier beers, too, which use unusual products—some of them local— such as Philsamic, made with balsamic vinegar; Kriek, aged with cherries grown in East Haddam; and Kreuze, which has the addition of honey from beehives they keep on the Two Roads property. However, the standard range of beers, available year-round—IPAs, pilsner, stout, saison—have bigger flavors and aromas than most local brews. Their large loft-like tasting room on the second floor, with the steel tanks poking through the floor from the brewery below, is a fun place to visit and taste their beers. Although they are busy, particularly on the weekends, the flow of traffic is well managed. They only admit people 21 years or older, so you cannot bring the kids. Bring your own food or check their website for the food truck schedule at the brewery. They offer tours Friday, Saturday, and Sunday; check the website for the schedule.

Willimantic Brewing Co., 967 Main St., Willimantic 06226; (860) 423-6777; willimanticbrewingcompany.com. Open Mon, 4 p.m. to 1 a.m.; Tue through Thurs and Sun, 11:30 a.m. to 1 am; Fri and Sat, 11:30 a.m. to 2 a.m. Owner and brewmaster Dan Wollner describes the building in which his brewery and restaurant is located as a "living landmark." He's certainly done a great job of giving this abandoned 1910 granite and limestone US Post Office Building—there are so many of these in Connecticut just left empty—new life. He's turned the building, which was left with no purpose for 30 years, into a beer hall and restaurant right in the center of this old industrial city. It's lots of fun to drink beer in what used to be the lobby of the post office, now filled with lots of mail service and beer memorabilia, with its big windows, high ceilings, plaster decorative frills, and marble floors. From the dining room, you can see, through the glass partition, where the company's beer is made—eight or nine different handcrafted brews per month. The wooden bar is one of the best and longest you'll cozy up to in Connecticut; the old customer service windows and personal mailboxes are still in place behind it. As you might imagine, the names of Willimantic Brewing Co.'s beers also carry the post office theme. Certified Gold is their signature golden ale, but there's also First Class Festive Ale and E-Mail IPA (both unfiltered IPAs), Hopped On It (bitter ale), and a long list of others, including Flowers Phunk, flavored with rose buds, hibiscus, lavender, chamomile, calendula, and clover honey. In the restaurant they offer a huge food selection and a long list of guest beers, many Connecticut made. It's a popular place with the locals and students from UConn, several miles away in Storrs, and Eastern Connecticut State University, whose campus is located just up the street. So be prepared for a noisy, raucous, but very friendly experience when the place is full.

Beverages (Non-alcoholic)

Avery's, 520 Corbin Ave., New Britain 06052; (860) 224-0830; averysoda.com. Open Tues through Wed, 8:30 a.m. to 5:30 p.m.; Thurs, 8:30 a.m. to 7 p.m.; Fri, 8:30 a.m. to 6 p.m.; Sat 8:30 a.m. to 3 p.m. They make soda at Avery's with pure well water and real sugar, not that awful corn sweetener. And they've been doing it since 1904 in the red barn on the property. When you pay them a visit you enter a crazy world of soda boxes, memorabilia, a 1950s-era mechanical bottling line, and boxes of soda piled up high in every corner. Founded by Sherman F. Avery, and now owned by Rob Metz, who is general manager, the company became known for what are today considered old-fashioned flavors of soda (birch beer, cream, and root beer), excellent home delivery (accomplished using horse and wagon the first 10 years of the company), and great customer service, things on which the company still prides itself. The soda is still packaged in glass bottles with labeling painted right on the glass, the business remains family owned, and just like Mr. Avery, who gave up his horse-drawn delivery truck for a motorized vehicle, the company continues to move with the times. While they still make those old-time soda flavors, their line of Totally Gross Sodas has put them on the modern map. Your kids will love them with names like Bug Barf, Dog Drool, Kitty Piddle, Monster Mucus, Swamp Juice, and Toxic Slime, the most repulsive looking blue soda with floating white things! But fear not, each has a delicious and recognizable fruit flavor! Or as they say on the website, "These totally gross flavors are dedicated to the 10-year-old in all of us." The kids will also like the company's Make Your Own Soda parties, which are held on most Saturdays by appointment. The kids are given a tour of the soda factory and encouraged to mix their own flavors. They get to take home three bottles of their own concoction and a soda maker's apron. Now what kid could resist that? And it's a clever bit of marketing, too, to introduce a new generation to this product that they might come back and buy throughout their lives.

Hosmer Mountain Soda

Hosmer Mountain Soda, 217 Mountain St., Willimantic 06226; (860) 423-1555 and 15 Spencer St., Manchester 06040; (860) 643-6923; hosmersoda.com. Open in Willimantic Mon through Sat, 9 a.m. to 6 p.m. Manchester summer hours are Tues, Wed, Fri, and Sat, 10:30 a.m. to 6 p.m.; Thurs, 10 a.m. to 9 p.m.; winter hours are Tues, Wed, Fri, and Sat, noon to 6 p.m.; Thurs, noon to 9 p.m. An old-fashioned soda company run by the Potvin family since 1958 (they are the fourth family to run the business originally started in 1912), this business was formed to supply the pure spring water obtained from Hosmer Mountain to the local mills in Willimantic. They make over 20 flavors of soda using naturally pure spring water; sweeteners (high-fructose corn sweetener or sugar); fruit acids; and natural flavors, including root beer, cream, white birch beer, and sarsaparilla (their "Antique Line"). Mixers for drinks, such as lime rickey and tonic; diet sodas in a dozen different flavors; special flavors, such as pink lemonade and ice tea; and a flavor of the month, which gets rotated and has included, among others, peach, chocolate cream, and strawberries 'n' cream are also produced. Soda is still bottled in glass, and, as their label designed in 1912 indicates, "in the Land of Swift Moving Water," the meaning of the Native American name for the city of Willimantic. Wooden packing cases have been traded for those produced from reusable fiber, and the company has come into modern times, most notably with the production of flavored seltzers and Red Lightning Energy Drink, made from pomegranate juice and grape skin. With both ingredients full of antioxidants, this product gives Red Bull and Monster a run for their money. The company has two retail "soda shacks," where you can purchase their products direct, but also offers home delivery (and they pick up returns!).

Simpson & Vail, 3 Quarry Rd., Brookfield 06804; (203) 775-0240; svtea.com. Open Mon through Fri, 9 a.m. to 5:30 p.m.; Sat 10 a.m. to 4 p.m.; closed Sat in July and August. When two employees of a Manhattan tea and coffee company, founded in 1904, purchased the company from their boss in 1924, Simpson & Vail, Inc. was formed. The business thrived in New York City in the Wall Street area for years. But when Jim and Joan Harron purchased it in 1978, among the significant changes they made was to move to Brookfield, Connecticut, placing their new shop against the natural setting of an old stone quarry. The selection of tea, coffee, and food items they offer is like no other you'll find in the state. The shop has an elegant European flair, and there are always a few pots of tea brewing. The merchandise is well organized and the staff is friendly, helpful, and really know their stuff. There's so much to choose from that it's difficult to make a decision, but the knowledgeable sales people will guide you through the impressive line of teas and coffees and offer great suggestions about what to take home. If it's a nice day, bring your lunch and wash it down with a cup of their tea in the gazebo, set against the pretty backdrop of the quarry. On Saturday from 10 a.m. to 4 p.m., they offer a free tasting of four teas and one coffee with fresh scones.

So. G Coffee Roasters, 882 Main St., South Glastonbury 06073; (860) 633-8500. Open Mon through Fri, 6 a.m. to 4:30 p.m.; Sat, 7 a.m. to 4:30 p.m.; Sun, 8 a.m. to 1 p.m. All you need to do to find this very cozy coffee spot in the center of South Glastonbury is follow your nose. The coffee is excellent (it's all roasted in the shop by owner Karen McRee using free-trade beans), the baristas are friendly and accommodating, and the atmosphere, both inside the shop and outside on the porch, is so relaxing that it's made this a local meeting place. If you still think you can't spot the place tucked into a small strip mall, just look for the locals who gather to chat at the tables out front on a sunny day. Wash down So. G's fresh baked goods—scones, bagels, muffins, pastries, and cookies—with some of the best coffee and tea you'll find anywhere. Don't forget to buy a bag of coffee roasted right in the middle of the room to take home, and ask them to grind it as you require at the cash desk. Customers inside get the extra benefit of the amazing aroma that fills the room when the coffee is being roasted and/or ground as they sit and enjoy their coffee. If you sit outside, you'll get the bonus of hearing all the local gossip or receive a recommendation for a good plumber or carpenter from the friendly, yet reputedly eccentric South Glastonbury locals comprised of farmers, small business owners, and artists. It is guaranteed you'll be back, and not for the coffee alone!

Ceramics/Pottery

Bantam Tileworks, 816 Bantam Rd., Bantam 06750; (860) 361-9306; bantamtileworks.com. Open Mon through Fri, 9:30 a.m. to 5 p.m.; Sat through Sun, 10 a.m. to 5 p.m. Former New Yorkers Darin Ronning and Travis Messinger have joined forces to make their handmade stoneware tiles and pottery, sold in a wide range of colors, in their Bantam studio and shop housed in a renovated pharmacy. They opened for business in 2004. Rich glazes, inspired by the glass tiles produced by Tiffany Studios in the 19th century, are the result of layers of luminous color and have become the signature work of this team. One hundred colors in eight different tile sizes are on offer and they also make tiles to special sizes. Their stoneware bowls and platters

would be enough reason to have a dinner party just to show off the colors, shapes, and patterns. Imagining the colorful things the deep purple, ruby red, and sapphire blue platters might hold is the only motivation required to purchase one of these beautiful exotic objects. And they are reasonably priced, too! These guys also make beautiful tile-topped tables, from small bedside to dining room, as well as game boards and trays. The whimsical bas-relief animal tiles—rabbits, turtles, elephants, fish, pigs—would give any tiled kitchen surface an unusual accent.

Clay Bodies Pottery, LLC, 59 School Ground Rd., Unit 4, Branford 06405; (203) 488-3772; claybodiespottery.com. Visit by appointment only. Jane Strauss Novick and Patricia Rist had very different career interests, but making handmade pottery is one thing they have in common. Their mutual interest in clay and making pottery brought them together to start their pottery studio in 2002. They rented an unfinished industrial space, designed and built walls and floors, rewired the place to suit their purposes, and opened their studio on two levels. The wheels and all the clay that gets shaped into their lovely pieces are on the lower floor, and upstairs is where they have their kilns, fire their work, do the glazing, and store their finished work. The downstairs area of the studio is cleaned, reorganized, and turned into a gallery once a year, when they open their studio to the general public and sell lots of their work. Throughout the rest of the year, these two women approach the medium in very different ways. Rist uses old pieces of crochet work, tatting, or embroidery, sometimes pieces her grandmother and great aunts produced long ago, to make impressions in the clay before she builds a dish or container. She likes to preserve the memory of these items in the clay. Novick loves the organic and earthy nature of clay when she makes her functional and decorative pottery. The colors of her glazes are rich, and the impressions she makes with natural and man-made objects in the clay makes you want to engage with the fired clay and trace those embellishments with a finger. Rist and Novick love visitors, so call them, set up an appointment, and go see their work. You probably won't leave the premises without buying one of their beautiful pieces, which have their personal stamps.

Cornwall Bridge Pottery Store, 415 Sharon Goshen Tpke. (Rte. 128 at the covered bridge), West Cornwall 06796; (860) 672-6545; cbpots.com. Open Sat and Sun, 11 a.m. to 5 p.m. This is one of those great spots, located just over one of Connecticut's classic wooden covered bridges built about 1864, where you can buy all kinds of high-quality handcrafted items for your home, produced by glassblowers, metalworkers, woodworkers, and potters, many of them Connecticut craftspeople. Todd Piker is the resident potter and brains behind the operation, which has been going since 1974. He's created a spacious and interesting shop that spreads over two floors, where he sells not only his own pottery, but that of others, including lamps, tableware, serving items, garden pots, and furniture. Visit the workshop with its 35-foot-long, wood-fired kiln, take a tour, and watch pottery being made. A walk over the West Cornwall Bridge that stretches across the Housatonic River and a poke around this great store will become an annual ritual, particularly if you go there in the autumn, as the change of colors in the trees in this stretch of the river is particularly spectacular each year.

D. Wilson Art Pottery & Design, West Hartford; (860) 778-1850; dwilsonart .com. Visit by appointment only. David Wilson met another potter in 2008 and decided, after learning how to work with clay, to leave his job in 2011 to just make pots. From his studio in part of his home he has turned out signature lines of pots and other items that can be found in interesting craft-promoting venues around the state, including high-end shops, boutiques, and craft fairs. Some of his best-known ceramic kitchen and tableware is decorated with his signature rabbit figures, while others are plain as day, but have a meaningful phrase or quote incised in the rim or somewhere else. Whether it's a bowl, a cup, a platter, or a decorative egg, Wilson's pottery makes anyone who picks it up feel happy. Many of his pieces look as if they were made by fairies, as they are so pretty, delicate, and fanciful, and full of references to familiar flora and fauna. Wilson is keen to make special pieces, so tell him about your idea and he will make it become something beautiful that you can hold in your hands and perhaps mark a significant occasion.

Embracing the Earth, 52 Tram Dr., Oxford 06478; (203) 446-7864; embracing theearth.com. Visit by appointment only. Tangelene Ramsey has been making pottery since the 1990s and began making glass pieces only a few years ago. She makes unique, colorful coffee mugs, plates, platters, and other serving objects, and she'll even customize them for you. She also makes glass pieces such as sun catchers, vases, and candle holders. She shows her work at The Gallery at 37 in Derby, but you can make an appointment to see the work she produces and visit her home studio, where she also gives classes geared to people who want to have a go at the pottery wheel, but don't have time to make a long commitment to more than a few sessions. Ramsey also holds classes for teenagers, and can organize a party for kids, a great idea for school groups, scouts, kids who attend summer camps, or for senior citizens. Ramsey's pottery lessons would be a great gift for a crafty person, and the result of one of these sessions could serve as a unique handmade gift for someone special.

Greenleaf Pottery, 240 Chapel Rd., South Windsor 06074; (860) 528-6090; greenleafpottery.net. Open Mon and Wed, 10 a.m. to 5 p.m.; Tue and Thurs, 10 a.m. to 9 p.m.; Fri, 10 a.m. to 7 p.m.; Sat, 10 a.m. to 2 p.m. John Macomber is the granddaddy of potters in Connecticut, as he has been making functional stoneware that you can use in the kitchen or at the table for almost four decades. He's been in business since 1975. He's taught this craft to a great number of successful and gifted potters from all over Connecticut and beyond. The pottery he makes is distinctive in its lightweight feeling, which makes it easier to handle if you are cooking or serving. Hit it with your finger and hear the lovely and distinctive sound of the ring! Visit his gallery to buy some of his products or to watch him and his students work, and you might just find that you too want to take a hands-on class from this Connecticut master. There are also classes offered at the studio for children ages 6 to 14, but Macomber does not teach those.

Wesleyan Potters, 350 South Main St., Middletown, 06457; (860) 344-0039; wesleyanpotters.com. Open Wed through Sat, 10 a.m. to 5 p.m.; Sun, noon to 4 p.m. Started in 1948 and housed since 1970 in a repurposed venetian blind factory, this non-profit cooperative artist guild was formed to teach and encourage the development of craft skills. Its classes for adults and children are its main reason for existing, but its gift shop and its annual sale held after Thanksgiving are great places to find one-of-a-kind, handmade ceramics, woven textiles, wooden toys and cutting boards, Christmas decorations, and jewelry—many of which are made by Connecticut artists. The range of items and prices is wide and the quality is high-grade. The bright open space where the annual winter sale is staged is a lovely spot to spend an hour examining beautiful objects made by local talent. The smaller gallery shop is full of affordable items, open year-round, and has a new selection of items to choose from all the time. The volunteer artists are friendly and love to talk about the work on display.

Cheese

Beltane Farm & Tasting House, 59 Taylor Bridge Rd., Lebanon 06249; (860) 887-4709; beltanefarm.com. Check the website for tasting and visiting hours. Paul Trubey, who owns this business, makes and sells goat cheese, raw goat milk, ricotta, and yogurt from four breeds of dairy goats on his farm in Lebanon, where he's been located since 2002. He has about 100 goats, and he loves it when visitors come and see how he works and raises his animals. Your kids will love it, too. Be careful when you drive into the farm as there are goats—all with names—and cats and a dog roaming freely around the property. If you pay attention to them, they'll follow you around. The chèvre that Trubey makes is produced in a plain version, but also flavored with black pepper, chives, dill, and herbes de Provence, which can be sampled and purchased in the pretty, rustic tasting house decorated with dried flowers and herbs. The wood-burning stove in the winter months adds just a little extra bit of charm. He also makes a creamy and fruity brie-like cheese called Danse de la Lune, and an aged nutty cheese, Harvest Moon. Beltane's Vespers, with a stripe of ash or herbes de Provence dividing the morning milk from the evening milk, is yet another cheese they sell. In December they make chocolate chèvre, which tastes like chocolate cheesecake, and is produced by folding melted semi-sweet chocolate made in Italy and a little honey into the cheese and then rolling the cheese in cocoa. Tastings are usually offered on Sundays in the early spring, but please check the website to be certain. Beltane Farm cheeses are a popular product at many of the weekly farmers' markets all over the state. After you visit the farm, if you feel you and the family might want to keep a goat or two, they offer a course on goat husbandry and cheesemaking. Trubey encourages visitors to wander around the property and bring a picnic when they visit. It's a lovely setting in which to spend an afternoon among the goats and other animals that wander around, and the little ones will especially love this place when the baby goats arrive in the early spring.

Cato Corner Farm, 178 Cato Corner Rd., Colchester 06415; (860) 537-3884; catocornerfarm.com. Open Fri and Sat, 10 a.m. to 4 p.m.; Sun, 11 a.m. to 4 p.m. Artisanal farmstead cheeses made from raw unpasteurized cow's milk are certainly worth driving many miles to find in Connecticut, particularly if the cheeses, about a dozen different kinds, are as good as those produced here. In fact, this mother and son team, Elisabeth MacAlister and Mark Gillman, make some of the best cheese produced in the United States, using milk from their herd of 40 mostly Jersey cows. You can usually spot the herd grazing in the pastures of this small farm between May 1 and October 31.

MacAlister began making cheese in 1997 to keep her dairy farm sustainable. She taught Gillman her skills after he quit his teaching job in 1999 to work with his mother. Cheesemaking is now his main role in the business, while his mother manages the farm, the animals, and the milking. Driving down the well-marked country road to the farm is like a trip back in time, as it looks like nothing has changed for centuries, and certainly not since the time of Cato Ransom, a freed slave and craftsman, who lived at Cato's Corner in about 1800. Pull into the farmyard, fairly muddy in winter, and just before you enter the no-frills sales room, take a whiff of the air filled with barnyard smells. It'll set you up for what you are about to experience when you taste this extraordinary selection of cheeses all made by hand, mostly following northern European traditions. Taste them all and take some home. You'll never forget the popular Bridgid's Abbey, the farm's bestseller, or the nutty Bloomsday, the delicious result, they are proud to admit, of a mistake in the cheese production. The rind of Drunk Monk is washed with brown ale from Willimantic Brewing Company, and Drunken Hooligan's with red wine and grape must from Priam Vineyard, just down the road. But if Cato Ransom Blue is available, take some home as a tribute to the man who gave this farm its name.

Cheese Boro Whey, American Velvet Factory, 22 Bayview Ave., Unit 47, Stonington 06378; (860) 235-9654; cheeseborowhey.com. Call for opening times. Ricotta, mozzarella, feta, quark, and farm cheese are the specialties of cheesemaker Jessa Page, who sells her handmade cheeses from a little shop at the back of Stonington's

Cheese Boro Whey

American Velvet Factory. Page's youthful, rosy, fresh-faced looks seem to make her the perfect candidate from central casting to do this work: She looks just like you'd imagine a lady cheesemaker should! She started the business with her brother, Nick Sullivan, a chef who works in a Rhode Island restaurant just down the road. Handcrafted at the back of the shop from local milk, the cheeses are creamy and fresh and full of barnyard flavors. Page's enthusiasm for cheese is contagious, and she will talk you into tasting and buying everything she sells. The cranberry walnut honey quark spread on warm toast is reason enough to find your way to this little business; the taste of that product turns breakfast into a healthy obsession.

Rustling Winds Stables and Creamery, 148 Canaan Mountain Rd., Falls Village 06031; (860) 824-7084; rustlingwind.com. Open daily, 8:30 a.m. to 4:30 p.m. Joan Lamothe started her cheese business in 1998 to help turn a larger profit on her small dairy farm located, along with a horse farm since 1965, on the 200 acres her family has owned since the late 1800s. It's located in a beautiful rural area with views of Canaan Mountain that are spectacular when the autumn colors change the foliage. With the help and expertise of her friend, British master cheesemaker Florence Brocklehurst, Lamothe turns out cheeses mostly made in the pressed British style from cow's milk. Varieties include a blue cheese, a Cheshire-style cheese, four versions of Wensleydale-style cheeses (plain, with herbs, with sundried tomatoes and basil, or garlic and celery seed), and a Sage Derby-style cheese. She also makes goat cheese, a soft goat cheese spread with herbs, and a pressed goat cheese. In addition to raw milk cheeses and raw Jersey cow milk, she sells jams, jellies, chutneys, pickles, relishes, maple sugar products, goat milk soap, and sweaters, mittens, and hats knitted by hand, mostly from the farm's sheep's wool. If you are lucky when you visit, you might spot Lamothe making cheese in the creamery next door to the shop to learn how it's all done.

Sweet Pea Cheese and House of Hayes Farm, 151 East St.; North Granby 06060; (860) 653-4157; sweetpeacheese.com. Open daily, 10 a.m. to 7 p.m. A family-run farm, owned by Stanley and Dorothy Hayes, members of the Hayes family has been involved in dairy farming since the 1820s. The farm was established on the present site in the 1950s, where they originally owned and milked 50 to 60 Guernsey cows, and today have 65 milking cows and 70 Saanen dairy goats. When you drive onto the property you can see this is very much a working farm. They make and sell fresh chèvre in many flavors (the orange honey chèvre is a winner), feta, cow and goat milk, chocolate milk, Greek-style goat milk yogurt, whole cow milk yogurt, and scented soaps made from goat milk. They sometimes sell cheese curds, and always have eggs from their own chickens. The small farm shop is situated right in the heart of the activity, and there's a whiff of goat in the air. It's fun to observe the cheesemaking process from the little window in the shop if you're lucky enough to arrive when this is happening. If you visit between Labor Day and Halloween, the kids will love the Hayes Corn Maze, which has become a local institution since it was started in 2005.

Chocolate

Bridgewater Chocolate Company, 559 Federal Rd., Brookfield 06804; (203) 775-2286; bridgewaterchocolate.com. Check website for hours of operation. Erik Landegren, a native of Sweden, built a reputation in Manhattan when he opened Aquavit restaurant serving Nordic cuisine. He then went on to start a chocolate business in Bridgewater in 1995. With Andrew Blauner, his business partner since 1999, Landegren creates Bridgewater's handmade chocolates, truffles, toffees, and other sweet treats, which have become so popular that the two now have retail stores in Brookfield (their factory store) and West Hartford. Their chocolate truffles have been described as the best in all the country. Pay them a visit and you can be the judge. If you visit the Brookfield shop, you can smell the chocolate as you approach. Just follow your nose and you'll be wowed by the flavors and velvety texture of the chocolate as soon as you take the first bite. It's great fun to pick a selection of chocolates in the company's attractive shops. A box makes a delicious and beautiful gift, gorgeously packed in a sturdy gold box with a bow and then slipped into a matching bag with a little gift card. Although the company has built its reputation on chocolate, you'll never taste toffee anywhere that is as good as this. They are pricey, but very much worth the indulgence.

Divine Treasures, 404 Middle Tpke. West, Manchester 06040; (860) 643-2552; dtchocolates.com. Open Sun through Tues, 11 a.m. to 6 p.m.; Wed through Thurs, 11 a.m. to 7 p.m.; Fri and Sat, 10 a.m. to 7 p.m. Diane Wagemann learned to make chocolates from her grandmother when she was growing up in Quebec. Today she uses Peruvian cocoa beans to make her own heavenly hand-made chocolate treats, which she sells and ships all over the country. Vegan dairy- and gluten-free chocolates are her specialty, as she uses no milk or white chocolate and only organic products. You will find truffles, bourbon-filled lips and hearts of chocolate, or even chocolates decorated with gold flakes in the shop attached to her chocolate factory at the back of her Manchester shop (which you can see through the window at the

Divine Treasures

sales counter). The finished products are all displayed in three cases in the small shop, and there are over 50 different types of chocolates from which to choose. Some of the more enticing are the combination of dark chocolate, blueberries, and hazelnuts; chocolate ganache, cinnamon, nutmeg, and cardamom; banana and macadamia nuts; or cranberries and pistachios. The ginger truffles, as well as Buddha's Blessing, shaped like a tiny Buddha figure and filled with mango, coconut, and spicy red pepper, are explosive in the mouth. The location in a strip mall is partly why her prices for top-quality chocolates are so affordable and, yes, dangerous, because once you've visited and purchased these gorgeous sweets, you'll rush back again and again to buy more. In addition to chocolates, she also sells a selection of other vegan products: cakes, cheese, ice cream, and other treats. She also sells sugar-free chocolates.

Thorncrest Farm & Milk House Chocolates, 280 Town Hill Rd., Goshen 06756; (860) 309-2545; milkhousechocolates.net. Summer hours: Thurs through Sat, 10 a.m. to 5 p.m.; Sun, 10 a.m. to 4 p.m.; winter hours: Fri and Sat, 10 a.m. to 5 p.m.; Sun, 10 a.m. to 4 p.m. Cows, their happiness, and the excellent milk they produce are at the center of this small family-run business. Kimberley Thorn, her husband, Clint, and her son Garret run Thorncrest Farm, where they have grown hay and pastured their herd of Holstein and Jersey cows since 2011. Right next to the barn is a tiny shop from which they sell their Fresh Cream Line Milk and Milk House Chocolates, which are made in small batches by hand. Kimberley's interest in making chocolates was sparked in Ireland, where she learned her craft, and was reinforced during a backpacking trip with her husband in Europe. With great care she chooses just the right milk and cream from a specific cow—she knows what kind of milk each individual cow can produce based on what it has been fed to provide the specific flavor and richness she requires for each type of chocolate. The results are extraordinary. Her chocolates are very different from anything you've ever tried. The chocolate is rich, but at the same time light and perks up your mouth; the flavorings in the fillings—mint, hazelnut, orange, raspberry, ginger, mango, rum— are distinct and linger on the palate. Short in stature with her little white cap, she looks like a milk maid/chocolatier who creates magic, but she will always give credit

Thorncrest Farm
& Milk House
Chocolates

to her beloved cows and respond, "The magic is in our milk." The chocolates she produces are simply unforgettable.

Tschudin Chocolates & Confections, 100 Riverview Center (at the corner of Main and Court Streets), Middletown 06457; (860) 759-2222; tschocolates.com. Open Thurs, 11 a.m. to 8 p.m.; Fri and Sat, 11 a.m. to 10 p.m.; Sun, 11:30 a.m. to 8 p.m. Rob Tschudin Lucheme is a lawyer in the morning and a chocolatier in the afternoon. If you arrive when he's making chocolates—you can call ahead to arrange this or for a lesson—be sure to join in on the fun. You'll find he's a character and quite a showman, tossing out one-liners and sound bites of wisdom about chocolate-making and other topics as he melts chocolate, massages gooey stuff, and forms sweet treats in the little kitchen behind the display cases. Lechume uses stone-ground chocolate and local honeys and herbs, but also mixes it up with some unorthodox flavors, including chocolates with fillings infused with Indian spices, Earl Grey tea, and even hot habanero chiles. Come up with an idea for a crazy centerpiece for a

party, and this guy will find a way to make it totally from chocolate, or choose from the chocolate high heels, flip-flops, running shoes, and ballet slippers on display. Hot chocolate is served in the good weather in the little cafe set up on the sidewalk outside. Customers are also encouraged to bring a bottle of champagne to enjoy with chocolate treats purchased in the shop. Or, bring the kids and check out the special entrance for the little ones that takes them through the production area so they can see how the work is done.

Clothing/Handbags/Accessories

BeeZ by Scranton, 1804 Boston Tpke., Coventry 06238; (860) 450-9240; beezbyscranton.com. Visit by appointment only. Why toss an old book that's beautifully designed when there's another very good use for it? Kathleen Scranton has come up with a great and very clever solution. She fashions vintage books—the covers, more specifically—into pocketbooks, wallets, electronics cases, and, if the book pages are in good enough shape, she rebinds those into a paperback and offers that to her customers as part of the price for her creation. It's one of the most interesting recycling ideas and crafting you'll ever come across. Each item is one of a kind and is reinforced, waterproofed, and padded to give the book materials new life. The end results are desirable, useful, and fun. Scranton uses beautiful and sturdy fabrics for the lining, gorgeous upholstery as trim, and antique buttons for the clasps, all chosen to complement and spotlight the graphics, colors, and designs of each book cover. The range of pocketbook styles makes it easy to get what you need. She makes large book covers into shoulder bags, with the straps adjusted to the correct lengths; handbags with wood, bamboo, beaded, or plastic handles; and clutches with handmade magnetic clasps and removable chains for straps. She also makes purses in which to carry your cell phone, tablet, or laptop. If you need a case in which to carry a sketchpad or want a lovely decorative box, she can make those, too.

The entire process of creating your book purse is collaborative. You can send Scranton a book or she can search for one you might like. She has an inventory of 3,000 books on her database, a link to which she'll send you so you can choose a book yourself. Once she has the book, she will send you choices with photos for the fabric, the handle style, the cord lip, and button, with photos and prices for each. You can also make an appointment to go and see her (or check the schedule on her website to see if she will be at a craft fair or flower show near you). When it's finished she will send you a photo, and once you've approved and made the payment she'll send you the finished purse and your paperbound book. She makes the entire process easy.

The Brothers Crisp, 1477 Park St., Ste. 2E, Hartford 06106; (860) 385-2040; thebrotherscrisp.com. Open Mon through Fri, 9 a.m. to 5 p.m. The moccasin—a very American shoe—is the model for the high-end, handmade shoes this company—which takes its name from the Saints Crispin and Crispinian, twin brothers and the patron saints of cobblers—makes in its shop located in an industrial loft in the Parkville section of Hartford. They have been making and selling moccasins that have been "revisited" since 2013, with American leather. The shoes have a very modern take that their customers seem to love. They sell what looks like a traditional moccasin, but they also make sneakers, dress shoes, and boots that have a hip moccasin feel with interesting touches of leather, different fabrics, and bold stitching. Made in very small batches, they are produced by a team—Joshua Westbrook and Jimi Maturano, the shoemakers, and Jeff Devereux, who handles the business side—in very limited editions, mostly for men, but with a model or two for women. The shoes sell very quickly, as they are so handsome and well made, and this all means that it will take about three to eight weeks to fill each order. They also take custom orders for shoes. Pay a visit to their loft and see how they do it by hand, the old-fashioned way.

Hardenco, 30 Bartholomew Ave., Hartford 06106; (860) 880-0495; hartforddenim company.com. Open Mon through Fri, 10 a.m. to 5 p.m.; Sat by appointment. Workwear is what this company sells—sturdy, well-made clothing in which to do hard work or, if you prefer, to just look good. The company was started by three friends, Luke Davis, Marshall Deming, and Dave Marcoux, who had the seemingly harebrained idea of making their own jeans, even though not one of them had ever sewn a piece of clothing in their lives. But they tried, working out of their family's three garages, and kept at it, and began making and wearing their handmade jeans. Soon their friends wanted to buy them, which created a demand. Their pipedream became a business in 2010. The jeans (in four styles), work aprons, and other items they sell are made by hand using antique sewing machines and mostly raw American denim and other fabric, thread, and hardware made in this country. And, they do it all in the basement of an old factory in the heart of Hartford, once an important manufacturing city. It's a small operation with only a handful of employees, but they make a first-class product. Each pair of jeans is a small cash investment, but with your purchase comes free repairs to the garment at any stage of its life. The thinking behind this policy is that if customers are wearing their garments for the purpose intended, there will certainly come a point when the jeans or other item will require a repair or two. This gives the company the chance to improve their work and to get to know their customers. Their ultimate goal is to make the best pair of jeans possible. What better way to do this than to get first-hand market research, which is also smart marketing when satisfied customers may just purchase another pair of their excellent jeans at the same time. For a small charge (check the website), they will also repair jeans made by other manufacturers and guarantee their repairs perennially. The travel bag they make from canvas is a mighty handsome piece of luggage and would make a great gift, but who can resist a pair of jeans with a leather label in the shape of the state of Connecticut? Hard to let that one pass you by if you are driving through Hartford.

Food

Arethusa Farm Dairy, 822 Bantam Rd., Bantam 06750; (860) 361-6600; arethusafarm.com. Open Tues and Wed, noon to 7 p.m.; Thurs and Sun, 10 a.m. to 7 p.m.; Fri and Sat, 10 a.m. to 8 p.m. If you are not careful, you'll drive right by the simple brick building that houses this chic dairy, as the parking is located behind the structure. The cows, which produce the milk at Arethusa Farm in Litchfield's rolling hills, are said to have a wonderful life, and that's probably why Arethusa sells "milk like it used to taste," as the company's website states. The milk from these happy cows is the key ingredient of the ice cream produced in many flavors (the strawberry or peach ice creams are the best selections), the yogurt, cheeses, butter, and eggnog (made during the Christmas season), all sold in the dairy along with the whole and skim milk from the farm. The farm and dairy are owned by George Malkemus and Anthony Yurgaitis, president and vice president of Manolo Blahnik North and South America respectively, the high-fashion brand of shoes. The range of cheeses is vaguely northern European in style: farmer's cheese; camembert; Europa (gouda-like); Crybaby (Swiss in style); Rotondo (stinky, but delicious); Bella Bantam (slightly tangy); and Tapping Reeve (similar to cheddar), named for the man who started the country's first law school in Litchfield, Connecticut, in the 1770s, and one of Aaron Burr's law instructors (Reeve was married to Burr's sister, and in 1814, was appointed Chief Justice of the US Supreme Court). The kids will like the window in the dairy shop from which they can watch the milk production in progress, the huge size of the ice cream cones, and the hot chocolate offered in the winter months. After your splurge at the dairy (all the products are pricey) you might just need a drink. Conveniently, there's a wine bar with excellent food right next door run by the same owners.

Bantam Bread Company, 853 Bantam Rd., Bantam 06750; (860) 567-2737; bantambread.com. Open Wed through Sat, 8:30 a.m. to 5:30 p.m.; Sun, 8:30 a.m. to 4 p.m. Patrons from as far away as Manhattan and Boston drive into the Litchfield hills to shop at this bakery. Started in 1996 by Niles Golovin and Susie Uruburu, the shop is housed in the basement of an old house. There's something about the setting, the view of the river out the windows, and the brick and stone building that evokes thoughts of rural France. Golovin is the baker and his main focus is producing excellent artisan bread from local small-batch producers: semolina batards, rye bread with caraway seeds, multigrain loaves, Irish soda bread, challah, and other types. The selection is large and the quality is well worth the drive. The rustic desserts—pies (including chocolate truffle and sour cherry), cookies (especially the soft ginger cookies)—are equally abundant if you arrive early before they sell out, and so delicious, also made with those local ingredients. The Dirt Bomb—a muffin with sugar and cinnamon topping—is the goal of many patrons who take the road trip, and it's impossible to eat one without devouring another. Once you've tried the products, you too will become one of the lemmings using this destination as a focus for a drive in the country.

PUMPKIN WALNUT

TEA CAKES
$5.00

MasterCard

VISA

Mrs. Clancy's
Irish Soda Bread

ntam Bread Company

Big Dipper Ice Cream Factory, 91 Waterbury Rd., Prospect 06712; (203) 758-3200; bigdipper.com. Open Mon through Fri noon to 9 p.m.; Sat and Sun 11 a.m. to 9 p.m. Harry Rowe III is the owner of this ice cream business, which his father started in 1986 and that he now runs with his mother. They use only top ingredients, which is immediately evident after the first taste of this luscious product. Their ice cream is creamy and smooth, with tons of flavor. They offer 32 flavors every day, made in small batches, including all the old favorites and plenty you always hoped to find or even dreamed of, such as coffee Oreo, banana walnut chip, cinnamon, or watermelon. However, toasted almond is truly their star and bestseller. The shop feels like an old-fashioned ice cream parlor with its friendly staff, little tables and chairs, and its collection of ice-cream implements and memorabilia. Be sure to bring a cooler when you visit; this is the best ice cream you'll ever eat so you'll need to take some home! And, if you give them two-days notice, they can produce an ice cream cake for you to take home.

Bishops Orchards Winery and Farm Market, 1355 Boston Post Rd. (Route 1), Guilford 06437; (866) 224-7467; bishopsorchardswinery.com. Open Mon through Sat, 8 a.m. to 7 p.m.; Sun, 9 a.m. to 6 p.m. The Bishop family practically invented the roadside farm stand in this seaside town, where their ancestor, John Bishop, came to settle from England in 1639. Members of the family have been running their farm stand since 1910, a year after their first orchard was planted, and it has expanded through the years to become a huge commercial farm market with 300 acres of farmland supplying the product. Six generations have worked the farm since 1871, when Walter Goodrich Bishop started the business, and each has helped the business evolve into a winery, bakery, farm shop, and grocery store with a large self-service prepared food section sold from refrigerators and freezers. Sadly a bit of the country charm has been lost, but the quality is still there. You can't miss the place, best known for their apples and apple cider, with the giant red apple above their sign, a local landmark, and their white "barn," which serves as their huge salesroom and is like a high-end supermarket. They also grow and sell pears, strawberries, blueberries, raspberries, peaches, pumpkins, asparagus, and

other vegetables as they come into season. If you prefer to pick your own products, they can offer you and your family the pleasure of spending a few hours doing that, too. Since 2005, they have produced fruit wines and hard ciders using their apples, peaches, pears, strawberries, blueberries, and raspberries, but they also sell the grape wines and hard ciders made by other Connecticut producers. They have probably the best selection of Connecticut-made alcoholic beverages found all in one place in the state. You can taste the wines they produce at their wine bar for a fee. Go in the autumn, as the shop is set against the backdrop of some of the best autumn colors you'll find anywhere in Connecticut. You can easily do your week's shopping here and find anything you'll need to feed your family, particularly during the growing season.

Black Forest Pastry Shop, 52 Lewis St., Greenwich 06830; (203) 629-9330; blackforestpastryshop.com. Open Mon through Sat, 7:30 a.m. to 6 p.m.; Sun, 8 a.m. to 1 p.m. Herb Mueller, whose parents started the business in 1982, and Dan Puffer invite customers to "stop by for a little slice of Germany." Herb took over the business from his parents in 1995 and has continued the family tradition of supplying pastries, cakes, and bakery items with a German twist all made by hand on the premises. However, Old World traditions aren't the only things visitors with a sweet tooth will find in this place. They also make their own gelato, chocolates, and own-brand Suitcase Jams. The variety of product is enormous. There's so much to choose from that when you visit, a great way to decide what to bring home is sampling a few sweet and delicious things, accompanied by an excellent cup of tea or coffee, in their cafe. The quality is excellent and the price is not too bad when you consider their location in the heart of up-scale Greenwich.

Buell's Orchard, 108 Crystal Pond Rd., Eastford 06242; (860) 974-1150; buellsorchard.com. Check the website for hours, which change with the seasons. The Buell family started fruit farming their land in 1889 when Henry Buell began tending the first orchards. The first farm had a small orchard, and Henry raised dairy cows and turkeys while also running a sawmill. Today it's still a family operation, and the fruit from their estimated 12,000 trees is so good that people drive from as far away as Rhode Island and Massachusetts to buy it from the fourth generation of Buells, Jeff and Jonathon Sandness (their mother Barbara was Henry Buell's granddaughter). There's a whole calendar full of home-grown fruit and other products they offer in the Quiet Corner of the state: strawberries in June, blueberries from mid-July to late August, peaches at the end of July to early September, apples from early September through October, and pumpkins from late September through October. You are invited to pick your own fruit, which can make

Buell's Orchard

for a fun day out with kids. They also sell vegetables, local jams, jellies, preserves, relishes, honey, maple syrup, and their own apple cider, but the word on the street is that they make the very best candied and caramel apples in the state. Check their website for the dates for their annual harvest festival always held in October. The kids will enjoy the old-fashioned hayrides and the live music.

Carmela's Pasta Shop, 338 Silas Deane Hwy., Wethersfield 06109; (860) 529-9533; carmelaspastashop.com. Open Mon through Sat, 9 a.m. to 5 p.m. Carmela Orfitelli, who came to the United States from a small town near Naples, Italy, when she was 17, makes fresh pasta, sauces, and Italian dishes on the premises of her tiny retail store in Wethersfield, which she opened in 1997. She and her sister Maria work in the kitchen, with its expensive Italian-made pasta machine, while her son Michael is the front man in the shop. Her business motto, "Serve your family what we serve our family," sums it all up. The business has been well supported by the local Italian-American community in Wethersfield and the nearby south end of Hartford. Customers can taste test the products in the small cafe at lunchtime with its six or so tables. Choose from the colorful selection of house specialties displayed in a glass case, and, if you like what you eat, bring some home! You can choose from 15 different kinds of handmade ravioli with a choice of wheat or regular pasta, and with fillings such as gorgonzola, pumpkin, roasted eggplant, or butternut squash; 17 types of fresh pasta; and 10 different sauces. If you prefer Carmela assemble your dinner so you can just pop it into the oven when you get home, there are six types of lasagna; manicotti; chicken, veal, or eggplant parmigiana; meatballs; vegetable side dishes; and dessert in the refrigerated display cases. The pasta is authentic with the chewy bite that guarantees you are eating the real deal. The prices are so good you will want to load up the car!

Dagmar's Desserts, 75 Main St., Old Saybrook 06475; (860) 661-4661; dagmars desserts.com. Open Tues through Fri, 8:30 a.m. to 5:30 p.m.; Sat, 8 a.m. to 5 p.m.; Sun, 8 a.m. to 1 p.m. There's a tiny piece of Germany and Austria in the North Cove Shops in Old Saybrook. The aromas from the kitchen will lead you to the door.

Follow your nose and go in and taste what Dagmar Ratensperger, the charming German owner, a native of Nuremberg, has to offer in the shop and cafe, which she opened in 2006. She will guide you through the delicious things displayed in her Old World bakery. Sample one of her amazing pastries with a cup of tea or coffee. When she moved to the United States in 1995, Ratensperger began baking German and Austrian desserts because she craved a taste from her native country and could not buy them in Connecticut. So she started baking them herself from family recipes. Her efforts turned into this delightful business. Sampling the fresh strudel hot out of the oven is a transforming experience: It's light and full of apple flavor, with the slightest hint of sweetness, which comes from the fruit. Holiday items such as stollen, *Gewürzkuchen Bienenstich,* or bee sting cake, with vanilla cream and caramelized almonds, are irresistible. But there are also dozens of other specialties, including *Käsekuchen*, cheesecake made with quark; *Donauwellenkuchen*, Danube waves cake, a marbled chocolate and vanilla cake with cherries; and *Schwarzwälder Kirschtorte* or Black Forest cake. It's impossible to walk into this pretty shop without taking something home.

Dee's One Smart Cookie, 398 Hebron Ave., Glastonbury 06033; (860) 633-8000; deesonesmartcookie.com. Open Mon, noon to 5 p.m.; Tues through Fri, 8:30 a.m. to 6 p.m.; Sat, 8:30 a.m. to 3 p.m. Owned by Diane "Dee" Kittle, this business was inspired by her own problems with celiac disease and her reaction to gluten. She opened one of New England's first non-GMO bakeries in 2008, housed is a little wooden cape with bright yellow interior walls, devoted to 100 percent production of gluten-free, dairy-free, tree nut–free, peanut-free, and soy-free products. The black bean brownies are unforgettable, but there are also chocolate mousse squares, magic bars, pumpkin pie bars, lemon bars, crumpets, snicker doodles, "Dee" doodles, and pizza. She also stocks gluten-free pasta brands and lots of other products that are top quality. And if all these healthy products don't help cure what ails you, have a chat with Dee. She's one of the most genuine and positive women you'll ever meet, the sweetest thing in the shop.

DiFiore Ravioli Shop, 556 Franklin Ave., Hartford 06114; (860) 296-1077; difioreravioli shop.com. Open Mon through Fri, 9 a.m. to 6 p.m.; Sat, 9 a.m. to 5 p.m.; Sun 10 a.m. to 4 p.m. DiFiore's is a family business that makes fresh pasta and specialty foods. Three generations of family members have been involved since Andy and Louise DiFiore opened in 1982, purchasing their pasta equipment from a Boston pasta company that went out of business. In 1984, they moved onto Franklin Avenue, the heart of Hartford's Little Italy, and today their son Don runs the store, which has become a fixture in the neighborhood, with his son Dan. They sell sauces, pastas, ravioli, and other prepared foods in Hartford's South End. They have many customers who have been coming there for years, who refuse to buy their pasta anywhere else, particularly when it comes to celebrations, which require

ata
5/lb

Bucatini
$ 3.95/lb
* vegan friendly *

Squid In
Cala mara-
H

pappardelle
$3.95

Spaghetti
$3.95

DiFiore Ravioli Shop

only high-quality pasta and other products. The place bustles and the pasta moves out of the shop quickly, so you can always be assured it's fresh.

The Dutch Epicure Shop, 491 Bantam Rd., Litchfield 06759; (860) 567-5586; alldutchfood.com. Open Wed through Sat, 9 a.m. to 5 p.m.; Sun, 9 a.m. to 2 p.m. Opened in 1967, this bakery and gourmet food store, specializing in Dutch foods and other products, is now run by Wilma Joas, who took it over from her father Wolfgang, a German-trained baker, and her mother Betsy, who was born in the Netherlands. The homemade cakes, breads, and pretzels Joas sells are made on the

premises from her father's German recipes and are a good enough reason to pay this place a visit. The atmosphere makes you feel as if you have been transported to Europe, and the display of cheeses, prepared meats, condiments, jams, jellies, sweets, teas, and many other grocery items are enough to make any homesick northern European feel so much better. Many brands, hard to find in the United States, let alone in Connecticut, can definitely be found in this shop. Joas selects them all on her trips to Europe. The pretzels made in the shop are what draw customers into the store on Saturdays, but the homemade soups, Hungarian goulash, and spaetzle are just about the best you'll find anywhere. Arrive early, as the lines get long and often they

run out of those excellent pretzels! But the staff is friendly and good-humored and will help you kill the time with their generosity of spirit. They also carry a large selection of Indonesian foods and condiments, in line with the other great cuisine, which is so much a part of Dutch life.

Eddy Farm, 851 Willard Ave., Newington 06111; (401) 932-2912; eddyfarmct .com. Open July through Oct; Mon through Fri, 10 a.m. to 6 p.m. (5 p.m. in the fall); Sat and Sun, 10 a.m. to 5 p.m. No pesticides, no herbicides, and no synthetic fertilizers is the rule on this family farm run by Andy and Haley Billipp since 2011, a business that has been owned by Haley's family since the early 1900s. The Eddy name was made famous, not only in Connecticut, but beyond, by Haley's grandfather, Roger W. Eddy, former state senator and representative, who invented the Audubon Bird Call, a small object that fits in your hand, made of wood and metal, that produces a bird-like sound when it is twisted. He used to sell these on the

farm. This is the only working farm in Newington, and it's located in the heart of town. The farm stand is full of just-picked, nutrient-dense vegetables during the growing season. They also sell their own honey. Just ask anyone in the town and they'll tell you that the corn they grow, in three different varieties, is the best around. They also sell 40 varieties of flowers on the stand, and bread supplied daily by the Hartford Baking Company. The flowers they grow are fantastic. They sell them in beautiful and unique bunches on the stand and they are in great demand, so visit the stand early. They will also make custom flower arrangements and can work with a tight budget if you mention what you can spend. They take pride in the quality of their products and thrive on the relationship they have with the local community.

Four Mile River Farm, 124 Four Mile River Rd., Old Lyme 06371; (860) 434-2378; fourmileriverfarm.com. Open daily, 8 a.m. to 6 p.m. During the summer and fall, they sometimes stay open until about 8 p.m. Nunzio and Irene Corsino started raising beef, pigs, and chickens on their farm in 1985, while by day Nunzio taught history in one of the local high schools. Today they are joined in this family operation by their children, Chris and Amanda. They take great pride in caring for their animals, and theirs is one of a handful of sources in Connecticut where consumers can purchase pasture-raised beef and eggs direct from a small local farmer. Their herd of Angus, Hereford, and Charolisis steer is small, so they can really look after them, and that care translates to the quality of the beef they sell. Their pigs, fed on grain and milk, thrive in open pens, and the eggs produced by their free-range chickens are the best you'll ever eat. They process the meat right on the farm. They offer any cut of beef imaginable, and they also sell their own uncooked meatballs, burgers, and meatloaf, as well as beef stock, all prepared on the farm. You can purchase frozen cuts of beef, ground beef, eggs, and sometimes smoked roast beef, smoked brisket, and smoked pork butt, as well as Irene's hooked rugs, at the farm stand. Call and find out what prepared foods they are selling each week; their cheeseburger pie, shepherd's pie, pork pie, and meatballs make a delicious and quick supper.

The Garlic Farm, 76 Simsbury Rd., West Granby 06090; (860) 264-5644; GarlicFarmCT.com. Open daily, 4th of July through "sometime in Oct," 10 a.m. to 6 p.m. As the name implies, this farm sells garlic, a variety called German White, and as you drive down the dirt road to their barn that's the first thing you'll smell when the garlic is in season. The garlic is harvested in July and then some of it is hung from the rafters of the farm's tobacco shed so that the ventilation can be controlled while it cures. Try to visit before October, as their garlic usually sells out by then. The braids of garlic they offer are decorative and provide the motivation to cook lots of garlic-infused recipes. Gary Cirullo is the farmer behind this magnificent bounty, using sustainable farming practices and no pesticides. He's been running his family farm since the 1990s and also sells seasonal vegetables, herbs, and flowers of the best quality at reasonable prices from the barn. You've never tasted tomatoes, potatoes, peppers, squash, onions, eggplant, leeks, corn, or basil this good. And on a hot summer day, the smell of the fresh basil almost out-does the smoky aroma of the garlic. So, buy both and make pesto. What is great about this place is that they guide you to the fresh-picked or recently harvested produce they sell, not that it really matters if you buy the day-old stuff, because the flavor is consistently delicious. And if a visit to the farm inspires you to grow your own, they'll sell you seed garlic and offer you some friendly tips on how to grow it.

Hay House Farm, 155 Ingham Hill Rd., Old Saybrook 06475; (860) 575-2387; hayhouseonline.blogspot.com. The farm stand is open Thurs, 2:30 to 6 p.m. Owned by artist and painter David Brown, Hay House Farm is a magical place with its house and barn constructed of hay bales (thus, its name) and stucco, with a cedar roof, pretty gardens, chickens, art studio, and yes, even its own stupa, a Buddhist shrine of peace and good intention. It is all set in a beautiful off-the-grid setting (there's no electricity and plumbing here), just a mile from the bustling center of Old Saybrook and the sea. Flowers, vegetables, jams, jellies, and eggs are for sale there depending on the season. Brown also sells his charming paintings. His paintings of his chickens are in big demand, so grab one if you can. He is better known as a portrait and landscape painter, but these colorful paintings, even with their poultry theme, have a great deal of sex-appeal. His garden paintings are also very desirable. They'd all look wonderful on the wall of any kitchen. If you'd like a tour of the property and all its interesting buildings, call and set up an appointment. Occasionally there's live music offered in this pretty setting and Brown invites the public, so check the website.

High Hill Orchard, 170 Fleming Rd., Meriden 06450; (203) 294-0276; highhillorchard.info. Open for the fall season Tues through Fri, noon to 6 p.m.; Sat and Sun, 10 a.m. to 5 p.m. Check website to see when they open for the season. Wayne Young, so say the locals, runs the very best farm stand in Connecticut. Getting there takes you a little off the beaten path, but what a bounty of good food items awaits the intrepid foodie, and the views of the fields—there are 69 acres of farmland—and the surrounding area are beautiful. The Young family believes in high quality, and they are very serious about providing good nutrition from the food they harvest, going to great lengths to be sure to only use natural minerals from the ground and ocean on their plants, trees, and soil. The difference in the flavor and look of their vegetables, fruit (more than nine varieties of apples, three types of pears, and peaches), flowers, and herbs is evident. The farm stand is no-frills and has an old-time charm. Pear cider is one of the more unusual items, which Young makes in the autumn, a rare find in this state, but refreshing and delicious. Their apple cider is considered the very best in the state. You can pick your own apples in the fall, an activity that is fun for the whole family or a great idea for a date.

Jones Family Farms and Jones Winery, 606 Walnut Tree Hill Rd., Shelton 06484; (203) 929-8425; jonesfamilyfarms.com. See website for seasonal opening hours. Six generations of Jones family members have been running this farm in Shelton, and it has evolved from a dairy farm to include Christmas trees in the 1940s (now growing on 200 acres), a harvest-your-own strawberries and blueberries operation in the 1960s, and a winery in 2004. They also grow pumpkins and have a farm education program with cooking classes for children and adults, and apprenticeships for those interested in learning about the farm-to-table business. It all happens in the beautiful rustic setting of this 400-acre farm, where locals make it an annual tradition to walk the hills and pick out the perfect Christmas tree, harvest their own fruit and pumpkins, and taste and buy some local wine. A visit with the family to buy a Christmas tree (either cut your own or buy a pre-cut one) in this gorgeous location is a fun way to kick-start the holiday season in November and December, when they also have a bonfire, cider, and a Christmas shop, from which they sell wreaths, greens, and homemade cookies. Picnicking is not allowed, but you can buy some cheese and crackers to accompany a glass of their wine. They charge a fee for tasting their wines, so check their website. The sparkling strawberry wine is delicious.

Joseph Preli Farm and Vineyard, 235 Hopewell Rd., South Glastonbury 06073; (860) 633-7333; josephprelifarm.com. Farm stand is open in season Fri through Sun, 8 a.m. to 6 p.m., check the website or call ahead for season dates. John Yushkewich and Jeanne Ellice have run this family farm since 2011, originally purchased by Yushkewich's grandparents, Joseph and Rose Preli, in 1920. It's nice to know that the Concord grapes they sell at the farm stand come from the vines that predated the Preli purchase of the land, grapes his grandparents always sold at the farm. The energy of this youthful couple to produce a quality product and provide great customer service is part of the charm of visiting. Many of Glastonbury's top-quality restaurants and the local Whole Foods Market, which brings lots of traffic to this gentrified farm town on the right bank of the Connecticut River, recognized it, too, and buy direct from this farm. If you call the farm to arrange it in advance, they'll even let you pick your own vegetables, a rare thing in this state. You can also pick your own blueberries, blackberries, and raspberries if you are so inclined. They grow fruit, vegetables, and herbs, including some unusual things you don't often find at Connecticut farm stands, such as Jerusalem artichokes, sunchokes, dandelion greens, okra, bok choy, tomatillos, squash blossoms, and nasturtiums. They also sell all the other things you'll generally find, but their selection of heirloom vegetables will have you coming back to buy all your fruit and vegetables because the flavor, varieties, and freshness just can't be beat.

Killam & Bassette Farmstead, LLC, 14 Tryon St., South Glastonbury 06073; (860) 833-0095; kandbfarmstead.com. Open daily, year-round, 9 a.m. to 6 p.m. Elder statesman Henry Killam, whose family bought this farm in the 1800s from the Hollister family, and Kevin and Chris Bassette and the five Bassette kids work this 85-acre farm in the flood plain of the Connecticut River. Pioneers in Connecticut's farmers' market circuit, they have become familiar faces at more than 26 of the markets located all over the state, selling their wide variety of farm-fresh products. The farm stand sits right next to the John Hollister house, built in 1675, the oldest standing house in Glastonbury. The stand, a simple wooden structure, is open year-round, using the honor system to sell fresh eggs, baked goods, honey, jams, jellies, pickles, fruit sauces, and relishes during the cold months, and all types of seasonal fruit, vegetables, and flowers, plus pork and chicken the rest of the year, all produced on this family-run farm. The meat products may also be purchased year-round by placing a call. In the spring and summer, the South Glastonbury locals use the stand as their grocery store, building meals around whatever is fresh that day. How about some grilled fresh asparagus topped with a sunny-side up egg, sprinkled with crispy bacon for supper, all purchased direct from the farm? Visit the stand and eat local like a local.

Lyman Orchards and Apple Barrel Market, 32 Reeds Gap Rd., Middlefield 06455; (860) 349-1793; lymanorchards.com. Open daily 9 a.m. to 6 p.m. The high-top apple pies made by hand are why many people return to shop at this farm market. People who have moved out of Connecticut come back every year to buy them for Thanksgiving celebrations, as the reputation of these pies is so solid! It's also a great place to do your grocery shopping and stock up on seasonal fruit and vegetables, apple cider, and almost anything you might need to feed your family. And if you like pie, you don't have to buy an apple pie, because they sell about 20 other varieties all baked on the premises. They feature lots of products made in Connecticut and New England, and if you prefer to pick your own fruit, you can do that, too. Bring the kids and pick berries, apples, peaches, nectarines, pears, and pumpkins. They have a great calendar on their website indicating what's in season and when you can pick. It's a great place to spend the day. You can have lunch outside at one of their picnic tables. They often have seasonal activities and events, and if they don't, there's plenty of room for the kids to run around to make room for a slice of Lyman's delicious pie.

Martin Rosol's, 45 Grove St., New Britain 06053; (860) 223-2707; martinrosolsinc .com. Open Mon and Tues, 7:30 a.m. to 2:30 p.m.; Wed through Fri, 7:30 a.m. to 4:30 p.m.; Sat, 7:30 a.m. to 12:30 p.m. The week before Easter customers line up out the door of Martin Rosol's salesroom to buy their "special recipe" Easter kielbasa. While many of the customers live in New Britain's Polish community, others come from miles away for this excellent specialty sold for just a few weeks in the spring. Originally started in a converted garage in 1928, the company moved to a new plant built by the Rosol family in 1948 on Grove Street, just off Broad Street. Customers here in the heart of New Britain's Polish community once had to enter the refrigerator room of the plant, with its saw dust floor, to sample and buy cold cuts, hot dogs, and Polish and butchered meat specialties. Three additions to the building later and the Rosol's still can't keep up with the demand for their products, well known in central Connecticut and beyond. In their attempt to keep up, they now sell their popular product online as well. But, if you get a chance to visit the shop, we encourage you to do so. The experience of standing in line with fans of the products is not to be missed. You'll not only hear all the local gossip, but you'll also get tips about what to buy, how to cook it, and hear stories from loyal customers about how they always looked forward to weekly trips to the refrigerator room to do the shopping with their parents when they were kids. Once you try this stuff you will be addicted. As one customer exclaimed: "It's not a holiday unless Martin Rosol's hotdogs and kielbasa are on the menu!"

Meadow Stone Farm, 199 Hartford Rd., Brooklyn 06234; (860) 774-4500; meadow stonefarm.com. Call or check the website for hours; closed in Jan and Feb. This was a chicken farm when Bob and Denise Noiseaux bought it in 1981. Their son, Kris, who now runs the property, made big changes when he took over in 2002.

He renovated the old farm building, added a bottling, milking, and feeding line to process the milk from the herd of Swiss Saanen dairy goats he introduced, and recycled some of the materials from the farm building to construct state-of-the-art cheesemaking rooms, where he makes artisanal cheeses and other products from the goat milk. After serious setbacks—the business lost all of its cheese during the long power outages following Hurricane Irene in 2011—this small family-run farm has come back fighting with a whole new selection of soft goat cheeses to add to the hard cheeses for which they have been known for some time. All made by hand from the milk, honey, and berries produced on the farm, the cheeses there are sold in the homey farm "shoppe" alongside Elsa's Suisse Kiss Skincare products, the handmade raw goat milk soaps and lotions they also produce from their milk and honey. Other products for sale are eggs, honey, bee pollen, and blueberries and raspberries in season. They also sell products in the shop produced by local craftspeople including lamps, jewelry, and beads. The kids will enjoy meeting Elsa, the matriarch of the pretty white herd of goats, who has lent her name to their line of skin care products.

Michele's Pies, 666 Main Ave., Norwalk 06851; (203) 354-7144; michelespies.com. Open Tues through Sat, 9 a.m. to 6:30 p.m.; Sun, 10 a.m. to 3 p.m. Michele Stuart has won countless National Pie Championships, and you can easily judge for yourself if her homemade pies are the best you've ever eaten. Her husband encouraged her to start a pie business after she won her first championship for her chocolate pecan bourbon pie in 2007, so fruit pies, pies with nuts, cream pies, savory pies, and other baked goods are what she has been selling in her shop since that year. Her pies are so good that many customers buy them instead of a birthday cake, plus she ships them all over the country. They are certainly for special occasions, as these delicious, handmade treats do not come cheaply. Cleverly, she offers some of her pies in smaller sizes. You can pop the smallest size into your mouth! The six-inch pies are a great thing to offer guests to take home after a dinner party, or a great solution to avoid a disagreement about what kind of pie to buy—just buy a few smaller ones and sample them all. And if someone in your family doesn't eat pie,

Michele also sells cookies, coffee cakes, and other delicious goodies that will appeal to almost anyone's sweet tooth. The savory pies are a great idea when you are too busy to cook lunch or supper; choose from several types of quiche, shepherd's pie, and chicken potpie—they're all delicious.

Nodine's Smokehouse, 39 North St. (Route 63), Goshen 06756; (860) 491-4009; nodinesmokehouse.com. Open Mon to Sat, 9 a.m. to 5 p.m.; Sun, 10 a.m. to 4 p.m. Right in the center of Goshen, Nodine's, which started as a small smokehouse in 1969, is tucked in the back of a property on which the impressive Nodine family homestead sits. As the sign indicates, drive behind the house, and the no-frills shop, which looks like a wooden shed, is located on the right. Despite the low-rent atmosphere, the place is full of smoked delicacies of a very high quality, all produced in small batches in the company's Torrington smokehouse. Smoked meats, fish, and cheeses are the specialties, smoked with natural smoke produced from burning hardwoods, such as apple, hickory, or maple. Among the treasures are the many varieties of smoked hams, ham hocks, bacon, smoked birds (chicken, turkey, duck, goose, Cornish game hens, and pheasant), as well as sausages (at least a dozen different types), cheese, and fish (trout, bluefish, and salmon). You can even buy smoked bones for your pet. The prices are high, but the quality is superior. They also have a deli counter where you can buy their sliced meats, soups, and baked products (including stuffed breads), or order a sandwich to go. If it's a nice day, have your lunch outside at one of their picnic tables. It's a little out of the way, but well worth the drive. Once you taste the bacon, you'll be back.

Red Bee Honey Apiary and Gardens, 77 Lyons Plain Rd., Weston 06883; (203) 226-4535; redbee.com. Visit by appointment only. Once the home of ballet dancers Gelsey Kirkland and Mikhail Baryshnikov, this property with its pretty red cottage and beautiful gardens in Weston was turned into an apiary by Marina Marchese, where she produces and sells her single-origin honeys. The honey produced at her apiary is wildflower honey, which is sold in several versions: the pure honey on its own; chunk honey, with a bit of the honeycomb in the jar; and Farmhouse

Honeycomb, the virgin honey still in its waxy honeycomb (you really can eat the wax). Additionally, Marchese sells under her Red Bee brand many other honeys made outside of Connecticut such as New York State clover honey, Georgia holly bush honey, Minnesota knapweed or star thistle honey, and many more. Participate in the "Talk, Tour and Honey Tastings," which take place out in the gardens, to find out how bees do their thing to produce honey and learn the differences in flavors and colors of the honey because of the different plants that are in season when the bees are visiting. You can also buy other bee-related products including beeswax candles, bee pollen, soaps, skin care products, T-shirts, and books in her little shop.

Red Rooster Gourmet Cookies, 16 Church St., Guilford 06437; (203) 533-4330; redroosterbaking.com. Open Tues through Sat, 9 a.m. to 6 p.m.; Sun, 9 a.m. to 3 p.m. Kimberley Welch sells nothing but high-quality cookies that are big, soft, and very tasty from her pretty yellow shop with its perky red rooster logo and open kitchen. This open plan means you can see where the baking magic takes place and watch how she does it. Bite into just one of her cookies and that taste will make you want to try each of the more than 40 kinds she bakes. The freshness and texture are seductive. Her local customers call Welsh a "cookie artist." Pay her a visit and see for yourself. There are a lot of cookies to choose from, such as raspberry white chocolate, Kahlua espresso bean, oatmeal butterscotchies, pumpkin dark chocolate chip, eggnog butter cookies, or maple bacon, just to tempt by naming a few. If you simply can't choose (often a problem), then buy a gift box of one, or two, or why not three dozen? The Red Rooster signature cookie is unforgettable: white chocolate, cranberries, butterscotch, and semi-sweet chocolate. It will leave you crowing like a rooster for another one! These cookies make great gifts in their handsome packaging tied with a big red bow.

Rogers Orchard, 336 Long Bottom Rd., Southington 06489; (860) 229-4240; rogersorchards.com. Check website for opening days and hours. Eight generations of fruit farmers have run this farm since 1809, with it's picturesque farm stand at the top of New Britain's reservoir. When Anson Merriman took the initiative to plant

1,000 Baldwin apple trees, he laid the foundation for the success of this farm, which now grows 20 varieties of apples, 10 types of peaches, and apricots, nectarines, pears, and plums. John Rogers now manages the business with the help of his family. It was his great-great-great-great-grandfather and Anson Merriman's father, Chauncey Merriman, who fought in the American Revolution and purchased the land to start this farm at the south end of the Shuttle Meadow Lake. Locals of all ages have taken part in the Sunday afternoon ritual of driving up the scenic roads with the family to buy fruit, seasonal vegetables, jams and jellies, eggs, and baked items at Rogers, a landmark in central Connecticut. The apples they sell set the measure for all other apples in Connecticut. Their apple cider donuts will make you euphoric with their flavor and lightness. Many families refuse to buy their peaches and sweet corn from any other farm stand. The stand has no frills; it's the real thing and it's very much worth a visit.

Rose's Berry Farm, 295 Matson Hill Rd., South Glastonbury 06073; (860) 633-7467; rosesberryfarm.com. Check the website for hours. Perched two-thirds of the way up Matson Hill (the locals call it "the hill") in a gorgeous part of South Glastonbury above the Connecticut River, you'll spot the well-organized farm shop tucked among the fruit trees and bushes of the Rose family farm. Sandi Rose is the current owner of this 100-acre farm, which began with only 20 acres in 1908 and has become an institution in this farm town. During the fruit season you can stroll through the property to pick your own apples, pears, blueberries, strawberries, raspberries, blackberries, currants, and pumpkins, and savor the view with its perfect light over the orchards on a sunny day. In fact, Rose's was one of the first farms to establish the tradition of picking your own products in the 1960s. Jams, vinegars, salsas, vegetables, pies and other baked goods, local honey, and Christmas trees and wreaths are also sold here, and if you visit on a Sunday, you can have a "breakfast with a view" on their deck. Check the website for other seasonal activities at Rose's, which might include hayrides, Halloween activities, or charity meals on the farm. And if you can't visit the farm, you'll find their presence at most of the large farmers' markets throughout the state.

The Spicemill, 191 Adams St., Manchester 06042; (888) 827-8985; espicemill.com. Open Mon through Fri, 9 a.m. to 5 p.m.; Sat, 10 a.m. to 3 p.m. A family-owned and -run business, opened in 1955, The Spicemill sells spices, seasonings, herbs, hot sauces, and cooking oils in bulk quantities to restaurants and the general public in a no-frills factory building, where they blend and package all the spices and seasonings. The prices are excellent, the products are fresh, and the knowledge of the staff is formidable. It's the sort of place where the accomplished home cook can find almost any culinary ingredient not easy to find elsewhere: saffron, truffle

oil, smoked kosher salt, sumac, whole nutmeg, a huge range of chilies—anything you can imagine, both mundane and exotic. Check the website for their monthly cooking classes, where trained chefs, mostly from Connecticut restaurants, will teach you how to use some of the products you can buy in this heaven-sent place for people who love to cook. The recipes on their website are a great inspiration to help plan a meal using your purchases, and there's a whole rack of them printed out and free located to the left of the door.

Stonington Seafood Harvester, Stonington Town Dock, 4 High St., Stonington 06378; (860) 535-8342. Open 24 hours a day, 7 days a week. Joe Bomster and his family sell the sweetest scallops you'll ever taste. He's single-handedly made this product famous, not only in Connecticut, but up and down the East Coast. He sells to top restaurants and professional cooks, as well as to the general public. What is so surprising to learn is that Bomster scallops are frozen—flash frozen on the boats and right where they are hauled in no more than an hour or so after they have been caught to lock in maximum freshness and flavor. Sound fishy? There's only one way to find out. Visit Joe's shop located on the working end of the fishing dock, past all the pretty houses in Stonington Borough. Bomster's father started the business in the 1970s, focusing on scallops with the help of his three sons who worked the boats with their dad. Today Joe has two scallop trawlers bringing in Atlantic scallops, and he supplies sixty to seventy restaurants from Massachusetts to Maryland, often making the deliveries himself. He's a busy man, but he always has the time when he's in his shop to talk to customers about his scallops, how he processes them, and how to cook them. He'll tell you that you don't need anything to cook a scallop if it's good. And if Joe's not there, you'll be charmed and delighted by the honor system set up to buy his product. Just select your pouch of scallops or other frozen delicacy from the sea (they also sell haddock, flounder, Key West pink shrimp, Georgia white shrimp, Maryland style crab cakes, Stonington stuffies or stuffed clams, soups, and chowders) out of the two freezer cases. Pay for it using the honor system: Just slip your money into the mail slot, rush home, and eat the best scallops you've ever tasted.

Stuart Family Farm Stand, 191 Northrup St. (off Route 133), Bridgewater 06752; (860) 355-0172; stuartfamilyfarm.com. Open Sat, 10 a.m. to 4 p.m.; Sun, noon to 4 p.m. Several generations of Stuarts have run this farm. Henry Stuart (grandfather of the current owner) was the first farmer in the family, and he began cattle and beef farming in Sherman in 1926. When the local government took over his property and 34 other pieces of land in 1929 to create Candlewood Lake by flooding the Rocky River Valley in support of big business (Connecticut Light and Power Company), Henry moved and began to farm in Bridgewater. Today it is still a family business run by Bill and Deb Stuart Jr. with their two sons Will and Christian. With 600 acres and 200 Red Angus cattle, they are kept very busy producing some of the best beef you can buy in Connecticut in one of the prettiest spots in the state. They also raise pigs and chickens and sell pork, poultry, and eggs and grow plenty of hay to feed their animals in the winter. The rest of the year, the animals roam freely on the land. If you need a pound of ground beef, a few steaks, or a side of beef for a party, they will prepare it, put it in a vacuum pack, and flash freeze it—all at a very affordable price. They can also sell you a small cut or a side of pork—75 to 85 pounds—which includes loin chops, spare ribs, a picnic shoulder, Boston butt, ham, bacon, and sausage. They'll deliver it for free, but it's more fun to visit the farm and the farm stand and pick it up. Their free-range chicken—the breed they raise is French Freedom Ranger—is exceptional.

Sugar Bakery, 422-424 Main St., East Haven 06512; (203) 469-0815; thesugarbakery .com. Open Mon through Wed and Sat, 9 a.m. to 5 p.m.; Thurs through Fri, 9 a.m. to 6 p.m. Carol Vollono and Brenda DePonte (mother and daughter) have run their bakery together since 2004, when it was originally called Mrs. Sweetza's, working out of their home kitchen baking cakes and cookies for local businesses. What a success they have become with their innovative take on sweet confections! Every cupcake, cookie, and cake they produce is full of flavor, not too sweet, and very moist. Their delicious products melt in your mouth. Their reputation has spread internationally since they won the Food Network's "Cupcake Wars" in 2010. This is a busy and bustling shop—they sell over 10,000 cupcakes in more than 30 varieties, 1,000 cookies, and dozens of custom-made cakes all in an average week—and it is very much worth a visit. The shop looks like a candy box painted in Tiffany blue with three whole cases of different types of cupcakes, and one devoted to cookies and lots of other sweet things, prettily packaged and displayed around the shop. And if you are a cupcake aficionado, oh, the wonders you will find here: chocolate salted caramel, toasted almond, pistachio, and s'mores. Sometimes they add maple bacon brittle, the Elvis (banana with peanut butter and jelly cream frosting), or Fluffernutter, just to name a few. Their hand-decorated cookies are like little works of art, and the custom cakes are so beautiful they take your breath away. These are not just pretty sweets; they taste fabulous, too! If you can't decide on one, bring

Sugar Bakery

home a cupcake bouquet (12 of their bestsellers in a signature box) or a tower of 32 in an easy-to-carry tiered box for a birthday or party. If you can't visit the shop to buy these delicious treats, look out for one of their Sugar food trucks that spread the good word around East Haven and beyond, usually found at special events throughout the state. Check the website for the food truck schedule.

Sweet Maria's, 159 Manor Ave., Waterbury 06705; (203) 755-3804; sweet-marias .com. Open Tues through Fri, 10 a.m. to 6 p.m.; Sat, 8 a.m. to 2 p.m.; Sun, 8 a.m. to noon. Maria Bruscino Sanchez, known as the "cookie diva," turned her part-time job and hobby into a thriving bakery. She runs one of the best in Connecticut, and not only are her cakes, cookies, and other baked items beautiful to look at, they are absolutely delicious, or, as her company motto indicates, her creations are "more than just another pretty cake." Through her talent and care, she has built a huge local customer base, and with her cookbooks, the first one pulling on her Italian roots and cookie recipes, she has also garnered a national reputation.

Opening her shop in the 1990s in the neighborhood in which she grew up, Sanchez put her Italian-American family—including her mother, father, husband, uncle, and cousins—to work. The business did so well that she moved to a larger space and now has more than 12 employees. The display of cakes, cupcakes, and cookies in the shop is mind-boggling. She makes the classics, such as red velvet, carrot, and German chocolate, as well as more exotic versions like chocolate mandarin or apricot mousse and peanut butter cup or cappuccino torte. Try some of the cupcakes if a large cake is too much. You'll go mad trying to choose just one or a few of them, as they are all colorful and enticing. Then, there are the famous cookies, the recipes for which made her an international baking star. They are simply the best!

Sweet Wind Farm, 339 South Rd., East Hartland 06027, (860) 653-2038; sweetwindfarm.net. Contact the company about opening times. Susan and Arlow Case began farming just after they were married in 1986. They now produce some of the best produce in Connecticut and have become famous for their maple syrup and other maple sugar–based products, such as granulated maple sugar, maple

FOOD **69**

candy, jelly, cream, and lollipops. Arlow learned to work with maple sugar from his family. During the sugaring season (mid-February to early April) you can usually find one of them boiling their harvest on Saturdays in their sugarhouse built in 2005, where you can purchase maple products year-round. They have a slideshow showing the steps in the process for making maple syrup, and they offer a tour of their sugarhouse as well, where it is fun to watch the process of boiling down the sap, smelling the maple steam, and tasting a sample, maybe on top of a scoop of fresh snow if you are lucky. They hold an annual Maple Festival on the second Saturday in March, where there are usually pancakes and other good things to eat, fresh maple syrup, and live music. From June to November their sugar shack becomes their farm stand, where they sell their vegetables, herbs, flowers, blueberries, and pumpkins, all grown without commercial fertilizers or chemical sprays. They also make and sell their own jams and jellies. The farm is in a lovely New England setting, a great destination if you need a ride in the country and a great way to observe and learn about one of the great New England winter traditions.

Swoon Bakery, 109 Danbury Rd., The Market Place at Copps Hill Commons, Ridgefield 06877; (203) 438-4326; swoonglutenfree.com. Open Tues through Sat, 10 a.m. to 5 p.m. A gluten- and nut-free bakery, Swoon was started in 2012 by the owners of The Cake Box, a traditional bakery also located in Ridgefield. Customers who know both often find that the gluten-free treats are even better than those sold in the original sister shop, but let's just say they are tied for first place. Swoon offers a large assortment of sweet things to eat in a very pretty shop with little tables where customers can indulge in the delicious products with a cup of tea or coffee. They have the knack of baking classic bakery items with a little twist. Their chocolate chip cookies are made with chunks of chocolate and plenty of sea salt, and have a chewy texture; they make a pumpkin teacake with a citrusy orange icing that is just the right sweet topping; monkey pizza is delicious and easy to eat (especially in the car—it will never make it home), as it just pulls apart. They sell a large selection of cupcakes, cakes (call to place your order), cookies, pizzas, and breads. It always feels like you are going to a party in that shop; the sales staff is friendly and everything they sell is colorful, beautifully presented, and inviting as well as fresh and delicious.

UConn Dairy Bar, 3636 Horsebarn Hill Rd. Ext, Storrs 06269; (860) 486-1021; dairybar.uconn.edu. Check the website for hours, which change throughout the year. Many in Connecticut (most of them students or graduates of this institution, of course!), consider the ice cream—more than two dozen flavors—produced by the University of Connecticut's agricultural students since 1953, to be the greatest of frozen treats. The ice cream, milk, cheese, eggs, and many other products sold at the dairy bar are produced from UConn's own cows and chickens and used in the kitchens that feed hungry students on campus, but they are also sold to the general public, students, and visitors to UConn. The sales room is decorated like an old-fashioned 1950s ice cream parlor with red and white tiles and seats at the counter. On a hot summer day, sitting outside at the picnic tables, there is no better place to be. Have a peek at the ice cream being made through the observation window when you visit the dairy bar, where they make it Monday through Friday from 11 a.m. to 2 p.m., and from the original recipe developed in the early 1900s. You can also tour the facility if you call ahead. When you visit, buy some of the Diced Green Chile Queso Blanco, the Dairy Bar's award-winning cheese. The Coffee Espresso Crunch ice cream is a winner, and the servings here are generous, so come with an appetite. After you fill up on ice cream take a walk to visit the cows to show your kids where the milk comes from as a great lesson in farm-to-table cuisine.

Wave Hill Breads Bakery, 30 High St., Norwalk 06851; (203) 762-9595; wavehillbreads.com. Open Sat, 10 a.m. to 2 p.m., or pick up orders on Wed until 1 p.m. at the back entrance. Authentic, handmade, French country–style bread and other products are produced by Mitch Rapoport and Margaret Sapir in this Norwalk bakery. Before they started their business, they tasted amazing bread served in a Vermont restaurant made by Gerard Rubaud, a master French baker, which inspired their own business. Encouraged by their son Jake to open a bakery, they trained with Rubaud and began making their amazing three-grain Pain de Campagne from flour, water, spelt, rye berries, sea salt, and yeast, in 2005. The pair became famous when critics called it "the best bread on the East Coast." The organic spelt and rye berries they use are stone-ground daily on the premises, and loaves are baked each morning except Tuesday. The bread is sold at the bakery as well as in several local markets and Connecticut farmers' markets, and served in dozens of restaurants. When they opened their shop in 2011, they began to make ciabatta with olives and a whole-grain, multigrain boule. They've since expanded their list of breads and also now make other products, including croissants, muffins, cookies, bread chips, stuffing, and croutons. On Saturday, visit them in their bakery with your kids. They'll show you around so you can see how the bread is made. Taste the bread hot out of the oven when you visit; after that experience, life will never be the same! P.S. Get there early, they always run out of bread!

Woodland Farm LLC, 615 Woodland St., South Glastonbury 06073; (860) 430-9942; www.woodlandfarmllc.com. Check website for opening hours. Harold and Arden Teveris cleared the land in the 1960s that Arden's grandfather, Albert Carini, purchased years before, and revived the old orchard by planting new fruit trees all over this property in the most beautiful location up on Matson Hill in South Glastonbury. For years they were helped by their extended family, including their son Pete and granddaughter Sara Pezzente, who was always an enthusiastic and knowledgeable presence for Connecticut-grown products at many of the farmers' markets in Connecticut. The Teverises have recently passed the reins of what is considered one of the best fruit farms in town to Pete and his family.

Woodland Farm is worth a visit, not only because the fruit is of the highest quality, but because the conversation and advice is the best you'll find in town. Their peaches, luscious and sweet, and the blueberries, with their tobacco finish and depth of flavor, like a good glass of shiraz, are famous locally for the excellence of the produce as well as for the great care the family takes to nurture their crops. Their cherries move fast because they are tasty and superior in quality, and their plums are juicy and remarkable in variety. Locals visit in the fall to buy the many types of apples and pears the Teverises grow, but also to taste Pete's unpasteurized cider, which is the best that will ever pass your lips. As you look over the orchards full of leafy trees as the sun is getting low over the river, you get a glimpse of what this farm town used to look like many years ago before gentrification took hold. This is God's country, and the Teveris family is doing great work by offering the very best this lovely piece of land will allow to be harvested.

Glass

Architectural Stained Glass, 211 Hartford Rd., Brooklyn 06234; (860) 774-7040; asgstudio.com. Visit by appointment only. This team of four, at last count, is one of the few helping to maintain the art and design of stained and leaded glass in Connecticut. Denise Noiseaux opened the business in 1987, and she and her team have been repairing, restoring, and designing windows for churches, synagogues, museums, and other business, all over eastern Connecticut, but also as far away as Stamford, Long Island, Manhattan, and Pennsylvania. You can see their work at the Chapel on the Thames in Groton, Evergreen Health Care in Stafford, and the Slater Museum in Norwich, to name a few. If you have an idea for a window or other glass element in your home or business, make an appointment and bring a sketch, a photo, a bit of wallpaper, a color sample, or just a vague idea with you. Sit down with Matt, the designer, who will show you some of the company's designs and then translate yours into a window or decorative element you will love.

Beach House Glass Beads, 4 Hill St., Westbrook 06498; (860) 339-5098; beach houseglassbeads.com. Visit by appointment only. Mary Anne DeLorenzo works in glass as a stained-glass artist. She makes beautiful Tiffany-style lamps, windows, and panels, but in the 1990s she became interested in making lamp work beads, which are formed from rods and tubes of glass that are heated with a gas torch. The beads are decorative and you can buy them to do your own beadwork, but she also makes jewelry from them. If her enthusiasm for bead making motivates you to learn more, she gives classes for beginners who would like to learn the craft.

Hot Spot Glass Studio, 112 Post Rd., Fairfield 06824; (203) 257-7958; www .hotspotglass.com. Visit by appointment. Dylan Cotton and Christopher DeMort are accomplished glass artists and teachers who have used their more than forty years of combined glass-blowing experience to open this studio and gallery. They have been active members of Connecticut's art community for many years, and now visitors are invited to watch the artists while they work with hot glass, which is a complicated exercise of heating, melting, twisting, and blowing. It's a lot of fun to watch and to listen to either of the owners enthuse about the work they do. The idea is to encourage visitors to buy the beautiful objects the artists make there (centerpieces, light fixtures, and commissions), but hopefully also to interest their audience in taking classes or workshops, which they offer here for both adults and young people, as well as rented studio time. If you take the beginning class you get to blow your own glass ornament.

JC ArtGlass Designs, LLC, 696 Main St., Branford 06405; (203) 481-0408; jcartglass.com. Visit by appointment only. Jayne Crowley works in glass from her studio restoring and making wall pieces, windows, doors, fireplace screens, clocks, plates, bowls, wall tiles, and other objects to sell in her shop and to customers for homes and businesses. Stained glass is her obsession and her life, and she has loved every minute of the time she's spent with the craft since she began to work in the medium in the 1970s. She is basically self-taught and works on all sorts of projects and in all sizes, from huge windows, doors, and panels, to small objects for the table and home. Her work is in great demand, probably because of its colorful stylized designs, often with a very modern approach to line and composition. Maybe you have an idea for a design in stained glass in your home? Crowley is an enthusiast when it comes to glass, and she could make something unique and beautiful from your idea. She sometimes teaches classes on making stained glass; check her website for information and be sure to sign up as soon as you see classes offered, as she's a popular teacher.

Peter Greenwood Glass Blowing Studio, 3 Robertsville Rd., Riverton 06065; (860) 738-9464; petergreenwood.com. Visit by appointment Tues through Sat. Admission is $25 per person and no more than 10 people are allowed per visit. Housed in the beautiful stone Union Episcopal Church, the first church built in Riverton in 1829, Peter Greenwood's studio on the first floor is an exciting space to visit, and a church building seems a perfect place for a glass blower to be working. Glass blowing is not the only craft he practices, as is evident after a visit to the showroom on the second floor of the building. There you can see the array of beautiful things Greenwood produces, including objects made of glass, metal, and wood; paintings; and jewelry. Glass lights and elaborate lighting fixtures; chairs, wall sculptures, and tables made of glass, wood, and metal or combinations of those materials are displayed in a beautiful space full of light. The elegant glass bowls, vases, and drinking glasses he produces transport the visitor to Venice in their style. Instruction, workshops, and tours are offered, along with other interesting events including live music occasionally. Check the website for more information.

Studio Jeffrey P'an, American Velvet Factory, 44 Meadow Ave., Stonington 06355; (860) 536-9274; studiojeffreypan.com. Open Mon through Sat, 10 a.m. to 5 p.m.; Sun, 11 a.m. to 4 p.m. Jeffrey P'an studied glassmaking in Murano, Italy, home to some of the greatest glass artists in history. He opened his studio in 1994 and makes unique, colorful, and intricate glass vessels, sculpture, windows, lighting, and glass and silver jewelry, which he sells in his gallery. The studio and gallery are filled with light and dozens of examples of all the different kinds of work he does. The jewelry is particularly desirable and affordable, and would make a unique gift, as no two pieces are alike, and it's very light in weight to wear. P'an gives glassblowing demonstrations on Tuesday, Thursday, and Saturday, so you can watch him work. He also takes commissions for lighting, windows, and sculptures. Any of his colorful pieces would make any room in your home or office dazzle. He's a tremendously creative craftsman.

Vasiloff Stained Glass Studio, 4-1 Craig Rd., Old Lyme 06371; (860) 434-9770; vasiloffstainedglass.com. Visit by appointment only. Marsha Vasiloff Abrahamson is a stained glass artist who works on a very large scale—one of the few Connecticut artists who still does that kind of work with glass—and also on smaller projects, producing wall dividers, windows, and lamps for homes, churches, rest homes, businesses, and other glass companies. She started the business with her late

Studio Jeffrey P'an

husband, Tony, whom she met when they both worked for a company in Old Saybrook that made and sold glass reproductions of Tiffany lamps. That's where she discovered the magic of working in glass. When they began the business, they worked from their home studio, where she now works, and then opened a shop in New London, which she has now closed. They built an international reputation for their glasswork. Perhaps the best example of the quality and scale of her work can be seen at the Foxwoods Resort Casino in Ledyard, where she designed and installed about 2,000 separate windows, three-dimensional pieces, and room and area dividers, using stained and etched glass, when the casino opened in 1992. The work took her 13 years to complete, and as the place expands, her work there continues. The beautiful floral designs in the casino concourse and gaming room, the backlit ones in the baccarat room, and many other fixtures throughout the large complex give a sense of her enormous creative and technical achievement. It's also easy to find her work all over Connecticut, including window restoration work in local churches and decorative windows in restaurants, as she is a perfectionist and her work is very much in demand. You might be able to identify her work from some of the images of the sea—she grew up in Westbrook—that she designs into her work. She is happy to take on commissions of any scale, so would love to talk about projects you might have for your home or business. Visit her and have a look at photos and samples of the large portfolio of work she has done.

Home Decor/Furniture

Chairigami, 55 Whitney Ave., New Haven 06510; (203) 747-8252; chairigami.com. Open Mon through Fri, 10:30 a.m. to 6 p.m. Zack Rotholz loves cardboard, a passion that began as a child playing in a refrigerator box, then grew from teaching kids to engineer cardboard, and later blossomed when he was employed as a mechanical engineer designing equipment for disabled children from that sturdy material. He took that enthusiasm for cardboard and turned it into a very clever business. As he puts it, "Now I'm ready to save the world, one cardboard chair at a time." He makes lightweight, durable cardboard furniture, which is easy to assemble and transport because it all folds flat. It's like origami using sturdy cardboard. All of his pieces are recyclable and inexpensive as well, so if you have a family that's growing or a business that's expanding, this is a great furniture solution. Rotholz sells the furniture ready to assemble from a flat package and provides very simple instructions. No glue or tools are required; you just slot it all together. It's all made in his shop and once you get it home it can be assembled in minutes. And if you don't like the brown flat surfaces, you can personalize it using duck tape, by cutting a hole for wires, inserting your speakers in the hollow spaces, or creating a colorful pattern to cover all that brown. It's a really excellent, affordable solution for students going off to college and so easy to ship and store.

CityBench, 73 Maple Ave., Higganum 06441; (860) 716-8111; city-bench.com. Visit by appointment only. Ted Esselstyn makes unique furniture by hand from trees that are cut down in city centers and other locations. Making furniture from wood from trees that can be identified gives the furniture a sense of place and attaches a story to each table, bench, or cabinet CityBench turns out. Joined in this work by his brother Zeb and Ben Komola, it is no surprise that they produce some of the most creative handcrafted furniture you'll find anywhere; this is a very talented team. Ted also works as an artist, Zeb is a journalist, and Ben is a sculptor who has also worked as an art conservator of monuments around the state and beyond. When a big tree needs to be taken down, it is highly likely that the team will be called to come and see it, and to help supervise the removal. They then transport it to their shop housed in three barns and get to the heart of it with their tools, creating the bare "canvas" slabs from which they coax their beautiful pieces of furniture. Their work is in demand, and by some well-known Connecticut businesses and institutions, including Yale University, ION Restaurant in Middletown, Choate-Rosemary Hall, Newman's Own, Bradley International Airport, Connecticut Historical Society, and local churches. The list is long and the work is recognizable, as you can always recognize a tree in the wood they use, and their work is evocative of the great tradition of Connecticut furniture making, updated to a contemporary style. If you need a special piece of furniture that is handmade, give them a call and arrange a visit to their showroom. You might spot something there that you will want to hand down for generations. Or, better, yet, tell them what you require and they will work with you to craft it. And if you have a great tree that needs to be taken down, you now know the routine and how to reach them.

Get Back, Inc., 27 Main St., Suite 4, Oakville 06779; (860) 274-9991; getbackinc .com. Visit by appointment. Designer Tim Byrne is the owner of this business, housed in an old mill, which sells original furniture designs and restored vintage American industrial furnishings or "vintage industrial/industrial modern," as he prefers to describe his products. The showroom occupies 5,000 square feet, so wear your good walking shoes, as there's a lot to see. He salvages and brings back to life pieces produced and used in America's industrial period, and turns them into one-of-a-kind keepsakes. Each piece feels like an authentic piece of American industrial history because it was used in offices and factories during the period of World War II and the post-war period. This was a time when solid, inexpensive business furniture was needed to support the business boom after the war, and very significantly so in Connecticut in the 1950s and 1960s. Many people who purchase Byne's repurposed and/or restored pieces buy this functional and aesthetically pleasing stuff for their homes and businesses. Sturdy swivel chairs, draftsman's tables, office furniture, storage cabinets, and lighting fixtures, mass-produced from inexpensive materials, fill the factory space. If you are looking for a piece of furniture once designed to do a job, but which also has an infusion of nostalgia for and history of industrial America tied to it, pay this interesting company a visit. You might be surprised at what you find, as it's packed with some real treasures. If you find something you really like and the size, color, or materials are just not right for your purposes, talk to Byrne; he might be able to adapt it, copy it, and remake it to the specifications you need. Let him resurrect a bit of solid craftsmanship of the Industrial Revolution from the graveyard for repurposing in your home or office.

James Redway Furniture Makers/The Silver Cherry, 87 Main St. North, Woodbury 06798; (888) 889-2723; redway.net. Open Sat, 10 a.m. to 5 p.m. Carrying on the tradition of making 18th-century American country-style plus 19th-century Shaker cherry furniture is a huge challenge, but the past runs through the blood of self-taught craftsman James Redway. An ancestor—an indentured servant with the same name and with no reading and writing skills—came to America in 1635. The company logo Redway uses (have a look at his web page) incorporates the symbol the first James Redway used to sign official documents, comprising one vertical line and three horizontal lines that cross it. Redway and his wife, Liza, who finishes each piece of furniture, have been producing high-quality tables, small chests, stools, quilt racks, wooden-edged mirrors, and other furniture based on early American models since 1986. They take no shortcuts, taking all the steps, beginning with the selection of the American black cherry planks from the lumberyard and "classic joinery that a traditional 18th/19th century furniture maker would to create a piece" of handcrafted furniture built to last centuries. Redway's creations are all on display in the little red colonial gallery he runs, where you can also find items he makes for the kitchen, such as cutting boards, mug trees, and cooking tools, including "The Redway Blade," a wooden spatula with a beveled edge. All this kitchen gear comes from the Redways' interest in food and cooking. They've produced a cookbook with 40 recipes or, as they refer to it, "the cookbook you actually use." It's also for sale in the gallery.

Reworx Collective, 30 Echo Lake Rd., Watertown, CT 06795; (860) 417-2858; reworxct.com. Visit by appointment only. This business comprises a collective of artists who work separately but with the same objective: to breathe life into old and found objects and materials. They have established themselves in a 19th-century textile mill, where lots of interesting work is going on, and their output can be seen in the studio and gallery displayed on several floors. Steve Garceau, who started Reworx, curates all the work the artists turn out. He's also one of

Reworx Collective

the craftsmen. Garceau works with an interesting group of artists, among them Frank Conroy, who makes green, sustainable furniture and art; Frank Lavoie, who makes chandeliers and table top lighting from driftwood and wood chewed by beavers; and Marlin Stevenson, a metal welder, just to name a few. Each collective member works to repurpose old wood, metal, industrial fixtures, found objects, or you-name-it into one-of-a-kind pieces. They also take commissions collectively to design a new house interior, a room, or an office, creating the lighting, furniture, and even the wall decoration. A visit to the company is like time-travelling back into the Industrial Revolution with all the machine gears, chunky pieces of wood, heavy metal fragments, and industrial and road signs, crafted or reinvented into interesting pieces with which you just might want to live.

Ruthann Olsson, Interior Arts & Design, Box 257, 20 John J. Curtis Rd., Norfolk 06058; (860) 542-5095; ruthannolssoninteriors.com. Visit by appointment only. Ruthann Olsson has a fine arts education, which she put to very good use, as she specializes in interior design since she started her business in the 1990s, She particularly focuses on creating painted interiors, including hand-painted architectural tromp l'oeuil bordering on canvas, which "tricks the eye." The borders are trimmed and ready to apply like wallpaper, a very easy way to spruce up a tired room. She specializes in custom work if you have special colors in mind. Olsson also produces beautiful painted paper and linen lampshades, and rugs, all in classic yet very contemporary styles and finished in gorgeous colors. The rugs, in two designs, are painted in acrylic pigments on a natural fiber base of jute, sisal, or a combination of the two. They are unique and could add elegance to any room. Make an appointment to visit the studio and have a look at her creations if you are looking to add a little sophistication that's unique to your home.

Troy Brook Visions, 38 Clark Rd., Litchfield 06759; (860) 567-2310; troybrook visions.com. Visit by appointment only. The husband and wife team of Daniel Gugnoni and Barbara Mojon Gugnoni make handcrafted furniture in their studio and gallery, which has been in business since 1993 in the Litchfield Hills of northwestern

Connecticut. When the couple married, Barbara came to work for the business in 1998. Daniel, who graduated from the University of Connecticut with a degree in sculpture, designs and makes the furniture. Barbara finishes each piece and handles all the marketing, sales, and customer contact. They have built a national reputation for making the kind of hand-made and finished custom furniture that families hand down for generations. They make chairs that are not only beautiful to look at, but comfortable to sit on as well; sturdy beds that are elegant and unique in design; desks and cabinets that look like works of art in any room; and dining room and side tables that are not only useful, but beautiful objects as well. They craft their furniture from hardwoods—mostly American cherry, Tiger maple, and walnut and mahogany from Africa, but they will use other types of wood if a customer requests it. If you have an idea about something functional, yet beautiful, for your home or business, furniture that might become part of your heritage, arrange a visit and talk to the Gugnonis about your idea and they will help you turn it into a piece of furniture worth cherishing. It will require approximately six months to design and craft your purchase. Also, watch for them at the key American furniture and craft shows across the country to see a sample of their offerings.

Jewelry

Carol & Company, 107 Main St., Collinsville 06019; (860) 693-1088; carolandcompany.us. Check the website for seasonal hours. Carol Ackerman is a gemologist and jewelry designer who set up her studio and shop in an old storefront building with large windows on Main Street in Collinsville. Many of the buildings in this area are reclaimed factory buildings due to the town's location on the Farmington River, where the power of its water once turned turbines for the manufacture of axes, picks, machetes, and other edged tools. Ackerman works

in her studio, which you can see through the picture window when you visit her shop. Her jewelry designs in gold, silver, and gemstones often have botanical themes, and they take the spotlight in her shop. She also sells the work of about 130 other American artists, many of them from Connecticut, who make jewelry, fiber art, ceramics, glass, and many other one-of-a-kind crafts. This pretty shop is a wonderful place to buy a special gift and to use as a starting point to visit the many antique and craft shops and artist studios in the town's historic mill district.

Dina Varano, 27 Main St., Chester 06412; (860) 526-8866; dinavarano .com. Open Tues through Fri, 11 a.m. to 6 p.m.; Sat, 10 a.m. to 6 p.m.; Sun 11 a.m. to 5 p.m. This gallery's front window, painted with a gold border, reflects the design of what's inside and puts a spell on Dina Varano's customers, drawing them in to see just what is happening inside this magical space. Nature is the inspiration for the jewelry, small sculptures, and charcoal and ink drawings Varano makes and sells in her gallery and studio on Chester's artsy Main Street. A graduate of Rhode Island School of Design, her pieces have a sketchy linear quality and are full of movement. The jewelry designs feel as if she has used semiprecious stones and metal—silver, gold, copper, brass—to create an impression of many of the things that can be seen in nature when you wander around this gorgeous

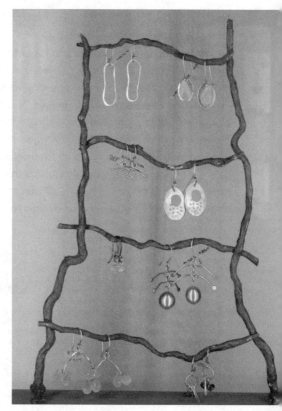

part of the Connecticut River Valley. The lightness of the designs makes you want to touch them and, most certainly, possess them! Creatively lit and displayed, among handbags, framed art, and scarves made by other artists, her jewelry takes center stage. A series of necklaces with emblematic stones and symbols, which the designer calls her "Talisman Collection," is displayed with their accompanying drawings under small Plexiglas boxes. Each piece in this special collection is sold with its drawing, providing a key to how this artist works and thinks.

Faye Kim Designs, 190 Main St., Westport 06880; (203) 226-3511; fayekimdesigns .com. Open Tues through Sat, 10 a.m. to 5:30 p.m. Faye Kim is a trained gemologist and goldsmith who worked in some of Manhattan's most prestigious jewelry stores, including Tiffany & Company, before starting her own jewelry design company in 2005. Her designs are unique, timeless, and distinctive because of her use of "granulation" when she works in gold. She attaches small discs of gold to the surface design without using solder, creating a sort of honeycomb effect, and often fills the little gold embellishments with gemstones, creating a rich and colorful design. When diamonds or pearls are used, they are perfect pieces of jewelry for any bride to wear on her big day. In addition to the various collections she produces, she is happy to work on commissions of pieces for special occasions. Bring her an idea and she will skillfully bring your design to life.

Metalwork/Pewter

Jeffrey Greene Metal Designs, 32 Church St., Woodbury 06798; jeffreygreene metaldesigns.com. Visit by appointment only. Jeff Greene has transferred his welding skills and knowledge of metals to those of an artist/craftsman and now makes beautiful metal objects in his studio. Inspired by Connecticut metal artists Alexander Calder and John Hallock, who tutored Greene, he found his own feet as a metal artist in the 1980s. He has built a reputation as a restorer of metal weathervanes and sculptures, creating one-of-a-kind weathervane designs of his own, interesting lighting fixtures, art, and useful objects for the home and garden from found metal, and anything you might think of that requires metal design. If you have an idea in mind, he'll work with you to produce it with knowledge and sensitivity to the metals he uses.

John Garret Thew, Norfolk 06058; (860) 542-5003; email: jthew@att.net. Visits by appointment only. John Garret Thew is a Connecticut folk artist who makes hand-hammered copper weathervanes. He began working with his father making decorative objects just after World War II in Westport, and then started making weathervanes just after he moved to Norfolk in 1972. Working from the small shop attached to his home, he has made more than 10,000 over the years, turning out three a week. Each one begins with a wood carving from which a mold is made. Thew places metal over the mold and hammers it into the shape of the figure, then he solders the metal parts together to create a three-dimensional decorative figure. Pigs, boats, birds, whales, horses, airplanes, and foxes are all part of his repertoire. The man and a dog in a canoe weathervane is particularly charming. If you've got an idea in your mind for a weathervane, he'll work with you to create it so you can add a New Engand tradition to your home or landscape.

Phoenix Welding, 122 Naubuc Ave. (at the rear of the Nap Brothers Building), Glastonbury 06033; (860) 657-9481. Visit by appointment only. Metal welder Ray Secunda's custom-made chairs, tables, bar rails, metal signs, food smokers, and fire pits are a fixture in Glastonbury's restaurants, homes, and gardens. Bring Secunda a piece of metal you found that you might like to see reused, a sketch or photo of a metal object you love, or one that needs repair, or just talk to him about what you dream of owning. If it can be made in metal, he'll figure it out. His shop at the back of the historic Nap Brothers Building is a little tough to find, but everyone in town knows Ray (he gives a Christmas party every December and most of the town turns up! He's also built a reputation in town for his expertise in smoking and barbecuing meat for his party!). Just ask any of the small business owners in the factory complex and they will show you where to find his shop. With its brick walls hung with tools and metal signs, and the pot-bellied stove he uses as the only heat source, you'll feel like you've time-traveled back to the early days when this building supplied the ship-building industry that thrived on this part of the Connecticut River in the early 19th century.

Woodbury Pewter, 860 Main St. South, Woodbury 06798; (203) 263-2668. Call to verify opening days and times. Starting out in 1952 in a small building that was once a blacksmith shop, Ruth Holbrook and Lee R. Titcomb built a local business using methods and tools from the 18th and 19th century to make reproductions of early American objects in pewter. Pewter making is a craft that was made popular in Connecticut by the Danforth family of Norwich beginning in 1733, and it was driven by five generations of craftspeople the family trained between the 1730s and 1840, building a reputation in the state for well-made pewter objects. Woodbury Pewter is now one of the few companies in the state to practice the craft. From money clips to napkin rings, corkscrews to dinnerware, drink stoppers, bowls and bells, trophies, tea and coffeepots, pitchers, vases, and porringers, if it can be made in pewter they can make it. They stock over 350 items made from pewter. Their factory outlet store also offers pewter objects made by 40 other manufacturers throughout the United States.

Miscellaneous Products

Carol Grave, 1298 Moose Hill Rd., Guilford 06437; (203) 314-8003; carolgrave
.com. Visit by appointment only. A weaver of colorful rugs, wall hangings, quilts,
clothing, and accessories that are a little out of the ordinary because of their design
and texture, Carol Grave began weaving in the 1970s. While she manages to pay for
her "weaving" habit through sales, she makes her interesting pieces much more for
the pleasure it gives her than for the cash. The juxtaposition of colors, the hot palette
she uses, and the unusual patterns she works into each piece make her work a bit
unusual among Connecticut weavers, as does the textural element she adds to the
surface. She sometimes recycles and mixes up materials and techniques to visually
challenge the repeated pattern of the weaving, and to break up the horizontal and
vertical qualities with which this craft is instilled. Particularly interesting are the rugs

she makes by recycling old clothes, and her "memory pieces" in which she mixes photos and clothing. These powerful pieces might be a great way to memorialize someone or a key event, and provide a soothing gift for a friend or relative who has lost a loved one or to preserve an important memory of something that happened in the course of life.

Comstock Ferre & Co, 263 Main St., Wethersfield 06109; (860) 571-6590; rareseeds.com/get-to-know-baker-creek/comstock-ferre. Check website for opening times. A 19th-century compound of brick buildings and barns all

interconnected to create a huge and meandering sales space has been turned into an unusual and inviting place to spend a few hours. The company's main business is selling their heirloom selection of garden seeds, which the company, despite several owners, has done for over 200 years. But, the seeds packed in colorful packets with gorgeous graphics and organized for easy access in old-fashioned wooden display cases, also set the tone for the other garden-related items and more that you'll find for sale here. Handmade soaps and skincare products, scented candles, fruit preserves and sauces, jewelry with a garden theme, pottery, clothing, antique furniture and household items, stationery, and prints and photos, are scattered throughout the building's museum-like setting. Many of the products are handmade by New England craftspeople, many living in Connecticut. Make a point of visiting in the early spring, as you'll find it difficult to find such an interesting selection of seeds for the garden anywhere else in the world.

Elizabeth Eakins Inc., 5 Taft St., South Norwalk 06854; (203) 831-9347; elizabeth eakins.com. Call for opening hours. After graduating from California College of Arts & Crafts, Elizabeth Eakins started a business making hand woven rugs in Soho in New York City in 1978. She relocated in the late 1980s to South Norwalk, Connecticut, where she has worked with her business partner, Scott Lethbridge, since 1981. From a large bright space with a design studio, a dyeing room (only environmentally friendly dyes are used) for yarn, a hand-weaving studio, assembly floor, and a showroom with a little boutique, she makes beautiful rugs from wool from New Zealand and from the small flock of sheep on her farm in Kansas. All of the work on the rugs is done by hand. The colors of the rugs are earth tones, natural colors that are filled with light. What is most interesting is that she can tell you precisely which animals her wool has come from in each rug. Her work—both her rugs and the fabrics she produces—is in great demand by top interior designers and architects all over the world, but she also sells to the general public. Visit her studio and watch the whole process of making a beautiful and unique rug. The showroom is full of samples of her work ready for visitors to buy, and, if you do purchase something, the product should last a lifetime.

Elizabeth Eakins

Folk Art Santas, 165 Hanover Rd., Newtown 06470; (203) 426-2927; folkartsantas .com. Visit by appointment only; check the website for times for their open house. Frank and Sandy Navone began their business selling carved and painted Santa Claus figures after Frank carved the first one as a gift for his wife in 1987. The next year they worked together to make figures for family members and friends as gifts, and it soon became a business. They now have built an international reputation for their colorful Santa figures made in a rustic folk art style, which are collected not just in Connecticut, but also by people all over the world. They do all the carving, painting, distressing, and antiquing of each figure by hand. Their busiest sales time of the year, naturally, is November and December, and that's when they open their charming home studio to the public. Folk Art Santas make great Christmas keepsakes and would fit into anyone's holiday traditions.

The Hartford Artisans Weaving Center, 40 Woodland St., Hartford 06105; (860) 727-5727; weavingcenter.org. Boutique is open Mon through Thurs, 10 a.m. to 4 p.m. In the mid-1990s, this center was set up to teach the craft of hand weaving to people over 55 and/or those who are visually impaired, but they have been operating in this space since 2008. This is a lively studio to poke your nose into when you visit the little shop. One senses that while learning their craft, the artisans who come to the center have created a wonderful sense of community and a happy environment in which they create beautiful woven pieces. Visitors can see samples of the hand-woven goods, including scarves, shawls, placemats, blankets, wall hangings, etc. These gorgeous creations are for sale in the center's shop and the sales contribute to running the center, along with the contributions and grants the center receives. The artists are also paid a small amount for everything they weave for the shop. Weaving lessons for middle school kids during the summer and for adults of any age throughout the year are also offered. Check their website for the details. The annual holiday open house and sale is a great place to buy gifts all made by hand.

Hartford Weaving Center

Heidi Howard, Maker & Painter, P.O. Box 112, Eastford 06281; (860) 974-3979; heidihoward.com. Visit by appointment only. When you've spent your entire life in New England and you are an artist, it seems entirely appropriate to take on one of the great New England folk art traditions to earn your keep. A native of Vermont and a graduate of Rhode Island School of Design, Heidi Howard, now living in a house built in 1780 and working in her garage in the northeast corner of the state, uses her talent to create trade and tavern signs in the style of 18th- and 19th-century sign painters of the region. In fact, her signs look so authentic because she uses 100- and 200-hundred-year-old hand-planed wooden boards and moldings she salvages, and hand-cut nails, and then paints and letters them by hand and distresses them to look aged. She's even started a side business of renting them to

Heidi Howard

film companies. Each sign is unique. She can copy an old sign or create something new based on your ideas. The objects and creatures she paints—beehives, shoes, mermaids, angels, American eagles, sea horses, owls, bulls, whales, and many more—seem to be perfectly matched to the words she letters by hand. American in spirit and lively and colorful, her signs have an authentically used and historical feeling. Even if you don't own a shop, a business, a tavern, or an inn, you'll want one to hang in a special place in your home or office. They are lovely and unique works of art, which speak of New England. They'd make a great gift for a lover of folk art or just this quaint corner of America.

Mystic Knotwork, 25 Cottrell St., Mystic 06355; (860) 889-3793; mysticknotwork .com. Open Mon through Thurs and Sat, 10 a.m. to 6 p.m.; Fri, 10 a.m. to 7 p.m.; Sun 1 to 6 p.m. Matt and Jill Beaudoin have turned a family tradition of making knotwork bracelets and other decorative items with a nautical twist from American grown and processed cotton rope or cord into a thriving craft business. Four generations of family members over a 60-year period have been practicing this craft tradition of tying knots and rope weaving, once the bailiwick of sailors. The business, located a stone's throw from Long Island Sound in a sail repair loft with views of the Mystic River, received a stamp of approval from Martha Stewart, in the form of her American Made Award in 2014. The products they make are rugged, of high quality, and beautiful in their simplicity. If you are a sailor, you'll find a useful selection of clips, lanyards, and even a keychain that floats, in different colors and knot patterns in their pretty shop. Bracelets, necklaces, or anklets are made in different widths, in more than a dozen colors, and in various patterns, and are great gifts for sailors. They also produce knotted collars for pets, and coasters, trivets, place card holders, woven mats, napkin rings, drawer pulls, and curtain tiebacks. Organizing a wedding by the sea and want a nautical theme? They make plenty of items that will help pull off the event elegantly. Visit them and they'll come up with plenty of ideas to transport the minds of your guests at your party a little closer to the sea with plenty of unique table items and gifts. Have a chat with the Beaudoins, who are very serious about their craft and heritage. You'll learn a great deal about

Mystic Knotwork

what they do and why, as well as a lot of local history. They are very much the real thing.

Nod Hill Soap, 81 Old Ridgefield Rd., Wilton 06897; (203) 210-5347; nodhillsoap .com. Open Tues through Fri, 10:30 a.m. to 3:30 p.m.; Sat, 10:30 a.m. to 2:30 p.m. Catherine Romer had no idea about how soap was made, but she knew she wanted to make it herself. She did her research and got her creative juices flowing to begin experimenting in her kitchen. Finally in 2012, she moved her soap business into a pretty boutique in Wilton where she sells fine milled bars of soap, as well as more rustic versions, body lotions, facial scrubs, lip butters, bath salts, face toners, room sprays, and drawer sachets in a large assortment of scents and sizes. The shop is as soothing as her products, full of light, soft music, and, of course, the homey, comforting scent of soap. It's a great place to find a small gift or to treat yourself to something that's luxurious, cleansing, and calming.

PEZ Candy Inc, USA, 35 Prindle Hill Rd., Orange 06477; (203) 795-0531; pez.com. Check website for hours, which are seasonal and subject to change at any time. Admission: children under 3 free; children over 3 and adults $4; admission includes a $2 credit for merchandise in the store that day. PEZ, the rectangular candy with a unique dispenser, has been produced in Connecticut since 1974, the year the company's New York City headquarters moved to Orange. Invented as a breath mint by Eduard Haas III, in Vienna, Austria, in 1928, the name comes from *pfefferminz*, the German word for "peppermint." The first PEZ dispenser, designed by Oscar Uxa, was produced in 1948 to look like a cigarette lighter to encourage people to stop smoking. There are plenty of things to see when you visit the facilities in Orange and you can even arrange a

party there. Take the self-guided tour and watch the production process through the viewing windows or video monitors to see how PEZ and the dispensers are manufactured. There's a display of memorabilia (cases of it, in fact, it's the most comprehensive in the world), which includes the largest PEZ dispenser and a PEZ motorcycle. Once you're done exploring, be sure to stop by the factory store and buy some PEZ and a new PEZ dispenser.

Shell Cottage Gallery, Lynda Susan Hennigan, 1089 Route 169, Woodstock 06281; (860) 315-5334; lyndasusanhennigan.com. Open most weekends, but phone for precise times. When she was a child of seven, Lynda Susan Hennigan was shown a sailor's valentine—an octagonal box filled with a mosaic made of shells—in a museum in Provincetown, Massachusetts. She was smitten and wanted to own one. However, the prices for these precious gifts made of seashells in Barbados between 1830 and 1880, and purchased by British and American sailors passing through Caribbean trade routes for their sweethearts, get high prices at auction today and are a much desired collectible. So, since she could not afford one, Hennigan decided to make them herself. She has a local wood craftsman make some of her boxes to which she applies a faux finish to make them look like original sailor's valentines. Her shell mosaics—incorporating sentimental messages, hearts, old ephemera, and nautical motifs— are all original, but patterned on 19th-century designs. The tabletops or dresser tops she designs are some of her most desirable pieces. What a sentimental and unusual wedding or anniversary gift these make. If you can't afford one—they are pricey—be sure you go and see them. They might inspire you to take one of Hennigan's classes so you can try to make one for someone you love.

Southwind Farms, 223 Morris Town Line Rd., Watertown 06795; (860) 274-9001; southwindfarms.com. Call for tour and shop hours. Jim and Penny Mullen started raising sheep on their 23-acre farm, but found that raising animals for meat was not to their liking. They shifted gears and now keep more than 50 alpacas on their large property, one of the largest Alpaca farms in Connecticut. They breed and sell their animals as well as alpaca products, such as yarn in 70 colors, clothing, teddy bears, and many other items suitable for gifts. Go and see these beautiful, photogenic creatures on the designated days the Mullens open the farm to the public.

Studio 80 + Sculpture Grounds, 80-1 Lyme St., Old Lyme 06371; (860) 434-5957; sculpturegrounds.com and gilbertboro.com. Visit by appointment only. Spread over 4.5 acres of land on the Lieutenant River, this "art park" is located in the historic center of Old Lyme, famous as the birthplace of American Impressionism. Gilbert V. Boro is the artist who conceived it and uses the grounds to display his abstract large-scale sculptural works inspired by nature, as well as works by other sculptors. There are over 90 works in the different gardens and courtyards on the property. Boro also designed Studio 80 on the grounds, with its loft gallery, where he works and displays more of his work. Large and small-scale sculptures and benches can be found throughout the grounds, which are open to the public. What's unique is that Boro has mounted his gigantic outdoor sculptures on metal plates with bearings beneath, which allow the visitor to turn the sculptures. Yes, you can move the sculptures, move under them, touch and stroke them; the art seems to invite you to do just that. In fact, that's the point of Boro's work: to engage the viewer to be a part of it, just as we each can do with many elements of nature. Poke your nose into Boro's studio, and if you are lucky, you might see him and/or his assistants working on one of his pieces. There's a nice place with tables and chairs to have a picnic or a break after a walk in the sculpture garden right next to Boro's home. Every work of art on the property is for sale, so ask for the prices if you are interested.

Studio 80 + Sculpture Grounds

Tucci Lumber Bat Co., 227 Wilson Ave., Norwalk 06854; (888) 810-2287; tlbats .com. Visit by appointment only. Tucci baseball bats are used by local teams, such as the Bridgeport Bluefish, whose Harbor Yard Stadium on Main Street can be seen off the highway when you pass by the Park City. Their primary business, however, is to supply professional bats to the big leagues all over the country. The high-quality ash and maple pieces of solid wood or billets they use are hand-cut and hand-selected, then burnished with hard steel to make the wood tough enough to withstand the hard-hitting they will endure on any baseball diamond. The company's owner, Pete Tucci, says, the result is "a ball that 'jumps' off the bat because, essentially, the wood doesn't 'give.'" Tucci was an accomplished athlete who played baseball at the college level, and then was drafted in 1996 by the Toronto Blue Jays, receiving the team's Player of the Year Award two years later. Traded to the San Diego Padres, his stellar career ended in 2001, after he lost power in his swing after a hand injury. To keep connected to the sport he adores, he started this company in 2009, and now makes the bats he used to swing for a living. Baseball junkies and players will be interested to know that the company makes custom bats as well, a great gift for an athlete in your family who might be thrilled to own a professional bat made to precise specifications for them. Call Tucci Lumber to make an appointment for you and your budding baseball star. It could be a once-in-a-lifetime experience, particularly for a player starting out in the game.

Musical Instruments

Fintar Guitars, 122 Naubuc Ave., Nap Brothers Building, Glastonbury 06033; (860) 944-5387. Visit by appointment only. John Johnston repairs cars, preferably classic American cars, for a living, but he's also a musician—a guitar player, in fact. He has built a reputation among classic car heads because he started drafting and making models for obsolete embellishments for their cars. One day, he sat down and brought his two interests together, using the drafting skills he learned at Glastonbury High School to sketch out a scale model of a dream guitar he had been imagining, with classic car features. He built the first of these fantastic looking guitars with a big shiny red fin, silver chrome trim, and red headlights, and it even has an exhaust pipe that spits out puffs of smoke, all modeled after a classic red 1959 Cadillac. He's also built a blue Flying V10 guitar modeled on a Harley motorcycle body. He's got many other ideas on the drawing board for more of these slick and elegant guitars, which he builds for some of Connecticut's best guitarists, including Jimmi Bell and Jay Jesse Johnson, whom aficionados

know from the local music scene. But you can have one of these guitars, which look like expensive pieces of pop art and have been road-tested by top musicians. Take your classic car out for a spin and pay Johnston a visit in Glastonbury. Tell him your fantasy or dream for a sleek classic-car-inspired instrument and he'll bring it to life for you.

Zuckermann Harpsichords International, 65 Cutler St., Stonington 06378; (860) 535-1715; zhi.net. Visit by appointment only. Richard Auber owns the largest harpsichord workshop in the United States, and it's located in Stonington. The business was started in the 1960s by German-born Wolfgang Zuckermann in New York City. When he began to generate too many orders for finished instruments, he invented a build-it-yourself harpsichord kit, known as the Z-box, soon discovering that he could make more money selling the kits than from delivering finished instruments. In the 1960s, when he sold the business to David Way, the workshop was moved to Stonington, and the business began to produce reproductions of antique instruments. The workshop established a reputation with top musicians internationally. Aubur took over the business when Way died in 1994. Four woodworkers make all the harpsichord parts by hand in one 10,000-square-foot room. Their work is noisy and makes it impossible for those assembling and tuning the instruments to do their work, so they work in two shifts. The woodworkers work in the morning and the finishers and musicians—artists-in-residence and harpsichord students, who are the tuners—take the afternoon. Today the company makes finished instruments, still sells kits, and does repairs on Zuckermann-produced instruments. A visit to the Stonington showroom, full of new and consigned instruments, will musically transport you back in time.

Paintings/Portraits/Collage

Lori Warner Studio/Gallery, 21 Main St., Chester 06412; (860) 322-4265; loriwarner.com. Check website for hours, which change with the seasons. Another graduate of Rhode Island School of Design and a native of Lyme, Connecticut, Lori Warner features guest artists and craftspeople in her large, well-lit gallery in the

Lori Warner Gallery

middle of the Chester artist's colony on Main Street. Her prints and encaustic (paint and wax) paintings tend to upstage their work, however. Her prints, composed of layers of ink and paper, which she describes as "woven monotypes," are stunning and filled with the brilliant colors of the sky, landscape, and sea of her hometown overlooking Long Island Sound. Additionally, there are lots of other references with New England origins incorporated into her work, such as boats, boat building, and quilting. On a limited basis, she will take on commissions for portraits or landscapes using your personal photo album as inspiration.

Madeline Falk Fine Art Paintings, Norfolk 06058; (860) 542-6929; madelinefalk .wordpress.com. Visits by appointment only. Connecticut native Madeline Falk is a dog lover (she owns four) with training in art from the Corcoran College of Art + Design. So it is a no-brainer that she would combine two passions to make a living as a painter of dog portraits. She's been painting these in oil and in a classical style inspired by the work of 19th-century European painters of dogs and other animals since 1989. Through the years she has won many prizes for her work, some of which is included in the permanent collection of the Corcoran Museum of Art in Washington, DC. Her paintings are full of light and detail, and it is quite apparent that she loves the subject she paints, a connection that allows her to capture the animal's personality. So, if you have a pet you adore and feel you'd like to keep its memory alive in a portrait, Falk is happy to accept commissions. She'll meet with you, photograph your dog, and paint its portrait, no matter the breed. She's probably the very best you'll find to do the job in Connecticut.

Paper/Stationery/Prints

Hartford Prints!, 42 Pratt St., Hartford 06103; (860) 578-8447; hartfordprints.com. Open Tues through Sat, 11 a.m. to 7 p.m. If ever a city needed cheerleaders, the city of Hartford has found three of them in the owners of this very cool shop, which specializes in, among other things, paper items with a Hartford and/or Connecticut theme. Three sisters—Addy and Rory Gale and Callie Gale Heilmann—run and operate this paper goods and letterpress studio, which they opened in 2013, in the heart of the state's capitol city. Their distinctive 19th-century shop front, painted turquoise, with its large windows, seems to draw visitors in to find out what exactly

is going on inside. The answer is plenty. The fun things they produce, from wedding invitations to greeting cards, are printed by hand right there on the premises on their Vandercook press. Visitors are encouraged to pick up a cup of coffee at the coffee shop next door and come in and browse through their collection of high quality, well-produced printed goods. Have a great idea for some personal stationery or an invitation to your next party? Well, bring it in and talk to them about it. They'll pull it together for you and make sure you have a lot of fun working with them, as they are a friendly and generous team of creative ladies. Their Hartford- and Connecticut-themed cards, notebooks, and T-shirts make terrific gifts. They also sell a number of items made in Connecticut by other companies and individuals, some with a Connecticut theme.

Kismet Letterpress, 123 Music Vale Rd., Salem, CT 06420; (860) 639-6598; kismetletterpress.com. Visit by appointment only. Artist, teacher, and graphic designer Dyan Gulovsen designs and prints unique wedding stationery; invitations; and business, note, and holiday cards on her two vintage letterpresses at affordable prices. Letterpresses, which make a very deep impression on paper, were once the backbone of Connecticut's printing industry. Gulovsen stumbled onto her presses, when she spotted a rusted-out one dumped on the roadside, over the Connecticut border in Rhode Island. She did

a U-turn, negotiated a price for two presses in much better shape, and had the heavy metal load hauled back to her garage in Salem, creating a new business and reviving this disappearing art. In her hands, graphics and images become works of art, particularly when she adds a touch of edge painting, all done by hand. Call ahead and visit the shop to see how printing used to be done.

Respond If You Please, 134 Main St. South, Bennett Square, Ste. 68F, Southbury 06488; (203) 217-8737; respondifyouplease.com. Open Tue through Thurs, and Sat, 11 a.m. to 3 p.m. Tiffany Boren, who studied illustration and design and has a passion for paper, has fulfilled her dream. She designs beautiful and memorable stationery—invitations, greeting cards, and other items—that are a cut above anything else you might find anywhere, and sells all these items from her charming boutique. Weddings and all the paper invitations and items that go into staging such a key event in anyone's life are her specialty. If you'd like to mark a special occasion in a memorable way, visit the shop, which opened in 2013. Boren will find a way to beautifully make your idea concrete and tangible, and walk you through dozens of interesting samples, types of paper, graphics, and embellishments. She'll make you feel like you have your own stationer. The selection of cards, stationery, and interesting gifts she sells will have you returning, and often.

Spirits (Alcoholic)

Hickory Ledges Farm & Distillery, 183 Bahre Corner Rd., Canton 06019; (860) 693-4039; hickoryledges.com. Visit by appointment only. Bill and Lynne Olson own a farm familiar to the locals for its apple cider made from apples supplied by Rogers Orchard in Southington, jams and salsas, flowers, and its new product, distilled alcoholic spirits. Yes, they make moonshine (legally!) from corn liquor, their apple cider, and some spices, and they call it Hickory Ledges Full Moonshine Apple Pie. Lynne describes it as, "grandma's apple pie—with a kick." Not only does it taste good, it's also natural and made right there on the farm along with other Full Moonshine products, including Pete's Maple "80," made from maple syrup; Cranberry, a blend of cranberry and apple cider; and other crafted distilled spirits. They have the right touch, achieving a great balance between local fruit and grain. They can't sell their moonshine on their premises, but they offer tastings and a tour of the production facilities. They'll tell you where you can buy the stuff nearby or in the dozens of liquor stores where it's in stock throughout Connecticut.

Onyx Moonshine, 64-D Oakland Ave.; East Hartford 06108; (860) 550-1939; onyxmoonshine.com. Visit by appointment only. When Adam von Gootkin and Pete Kowalczyk met at a party, they found they shared a passion and opened a recording studio together in an old wool mill, which dates from the American Civil War, in East Hartford. Onyx Sound has become one of the top recording studios in New England. As if that success were not enough, they used the name of their successful business to tap another of their passions. Billing their product as "New England's first legal moonshine since Prohibition," they launched their next business in 2011. Made from corn, malted grains, and Connecticut spring water, Onyx Moonshine is a smooth, clean alcoholic spirit, which packs a big punch at 80 proof. Perhaps the idea for this second business runs in their blood. Adam's great-grandfather ran a speakeasy in the basement of a hotel in Middletown on the Connecticut River during the Prohibition era; Pete's family grew corn on their farm in New Britain for 100 years and his great-grandmother supposedly had a secret place in the stairway of her house where you could leave payment for a bottle of moonshine that would be left in its place. Today instead of making moonshine secretly by the light of the moon, this young team does it legally in their small distillery, and it's all done by hand.

Wine

Chamard Vineyards, 115 Cow Hill Rd., Clinton 06413; (860) 664-0299; chamard .com. The tasting room is open Mon through Sat, 11 a.m. to 9 p.m.; Sun, 11 a.m. to 8 p.m.; bistro is open Mon through Sat, noon to 9 p.m.; Sun, 11 a.m. to 8 p.m. Check the website for specials and happy hour details. This pretty vineyard, with its 20 acres of vines, pond, vegetable gardens, and a winery constructed from fieldstones and wood beams from trees cleared from the property, was established in 1983 by Chairman and CEO of Tiffany and Co. William R. Chaney and his family. Owned by Bonnie and Jonathan Rothberg now, they produce about 6,000 cases of wine per year (they import grapes from other wine regions and grow some of their own), so there's plenty of wine stock to purchase and bring home. The vineyard is strategically planted on land that benefits from the microclimate created from its position six miles from the mouth of the Connecticut River and two miles inland from Long Island Sound. Mild temperatures in winter and a long growing season create a grape-growing environment similar to the conditions found in the Burgundy region of France. The attractive tasting room with its huge bar is a lovely place to spend some time sampling Chamard's wines, accompanied by some food from its bistro, with its French-inspired, farm-to-table menu. Sitting on your perch at the bar, where there's a charge for the tasting, it feels as if you are sitting right in the middle of the vineyards and gardens because of all the windows in the room. If the wine—Cabernet Franc, Cabernet Sauvignon, Chardonnay, Merlot, and Pinot Noir— goes to your head, you are free to stroll the grounds and inspect the vines yourself. You can also walk your dog on a leash out there among the grapes, vegetables, and flowers. The company offers tours of their facility for a fee of $20 per person for 10 (minimum) to 50 guests. Tours must be scheduled two weeks in advance of the visit.

Chamard Vineyards

Connecticut Valley Winery, 1480 Litchfield Tpke. (Route 202), New Hartford 06057; (860) 489-9463; ctvalleywinery.com. Check website for opening times. Anthony and Judith Ferraro, a husband and wife team, have been making wine in Litchfield County since 2005. They grow more than a dozen types of grapes on their 30-acre property. They produce a dozen or so red, white, and dessert wines (some from fruit other than grapes) each season. The family is confident about their wines, made evident in the tastings they handle in the gray barn that serves as their tasting room. They have won dozens of awards and much acclaim for their wines. The tasting room has an Old World flavor and is large with pretty views of the vines and the surrounding hills. Bring some food and enjoy your meal on the deck, patio, or in front of the fireplace. Drinking a glass in the setting in which it is made somehow makes it taste better.

DiGrazia Vineyards, 131 Tower Rd., Brookfield 06804; (203) 775-1616; digrazia .com. Open daily, May through Dec, 11 a.m. to 5 p.m. Call to visit at other times by appointment. Owned by Dr. Paul DiGrazia and his wife, Barbara, this business started in their garage in 1978, where the doctor made four different wines the first year from grapes planted on 20 acres in Amenia, New York. Still family run, the business now has half an acre of Niagra grapes in Brookfield near the winery and has expanded to 40 acres of vines in New York State. Honey blush (no sulfites!) and Wild Blue (port) are just two of the wide range of wines they produce and sell from their tasting room right next to their house in Brookfield. They also make fruit wines from pears, pomegranate, apples, and blueberries, and they add honey, brandy, sugar pumpkin, raspberries, and spices to some of their grape-based wines. A tasting costs $8 for six wines, or $10 for eight wines. Bring a picnic, buy a bottle, and eat lunch under the pretty grape arbor. It's a lovely spot in which to sit outside and enjoy your meal. Ask one of the staff for a tour of the facilities—they are friendly and accommodating. And they are dog friendly, too.

Gouveia Vineyards, 1339 Whirlwind Hill Rd., Wallingford 06492; gouveiavineyards .com. Check website for seasonal opening hours. Joe and Lucy Gouveia planted their vines by hand in 1999 and opened their winery, inspired by Joe's Portuguese roots and the wine-making tradition of his native country, up on a hill that catches the sun on bright days. It is a beautiful place to visit with 360-degree views of the vines, their pond, and the countryside beyond their property in the distance. They make 11 different wines, including whites, reds, a rosé, and a red dessert wine, and they grow 15 types of grapes on 32 acres. Check the website for the tasting fee. They offer tours of the cellars generally on Saturday and Sunday afternoons between 2 and 4 p.m. They have lots of tables for picnicking on the grounds, and plenty of seating inside. While they invite guests to bring their own food, they also have a supply of local restaurant menus for places that will deliver food to the

Gouveia Vineyards

vineyard. Weekends are very busy, so it's better to go on a weekday if you prefer to avoid the crowds. Visitors are not allowed to bring any beverages, including water, onto the property.

Haight-Brown Vineyards, 29 Chestnut Hill Rd., Litchfield 06759; (860) 567-4045; haightvineyards.com. Check the website for opening times. Among the growing number of wine producers in Connecticut, Haight-Brown Vineyards distinguishes itself by being the oldest in the state to grow Chardonnay and Riesling grapes. Starting in 1975 as Haight Vineyards, the business was purchased in 2007 by Amy Senew and Courtney Brown and renamed. Today the company has over 20 acres of vineyards, which it grows and leases. In 2014, they hired a new winemaker, Jacques van der Vyver, who was born and educated in South Africa, and who has worked for winemakers in South Africa, Maryland, and California. The setting on Chestnut Hill is very pretty, and the winery facilities—a large tasting room, a patio with a view, a terrace, two fireplaces, and a picnic grove among the vines—make it a great place to visit out in the middle of the country, no matter the weather. They offer tastings of their wines—Chardonnay, Riesling, two additional whites, two red wines, plus two made from apples and honey, and apples and cranberries—for a fee. Check the website for the tasting costs. They have a nice selection of bread, crackers, cheeses, and pâtés if you prefer to buy your picnic in their shop. Some advice: If it's a sunny day, arrive early. This place gets very busy, but the wines are well worth a little wait in line.

Holmberg Orchards & Winery, 12 Orchard Ln., Gales Ferry 06335; (860) 464-7305; holmbergwinery.com. Check website for winery and farm market hours. A combination winery and orchard, this is a family-run business started by Swedish immigrants Adolph and Hulda Holmberg in 1896 as a truck farm to grow vegetables and garden plants. When the Holmbergs' sons purchased the farm from their parents in 1931, the farm was also a successful egg producer, and the first apple trees were planted in 1935. The farm has been going strong for four generations. They now have 50 acres of land with orchards, vineyards, vegetable fields, and berry bushes. You can pick your own strawberries, blueberries, apples, plums, nectarines, peaches, and pears in season or you can buy your fruit and other items, including baked goods and vegetables, in their farm market. They also sell a wide variety of gourmet specialty foods and items made by local producers in their shop. Their apple or pear ciders are known for their quality locally. Winemaking is a new aspect of the business, which was conceived by Russell Holmberg. While he was studying for his agricultural degree at the University of Connecticut, his organic chemistry professor taught him to make wine. After college he returned home in 2006 and began to tend the family vines and make wine. Recorded on the wine labels is some of the history of the Holmberg family business. The first grape wine was made from Vidal Blanc grapes shipped in from New York state. The first estate-produced grape wine is the Pinot Blanc. They make wine as well from their own Gewurztraminer grapes planted in 2014. Russell makes a long list of wines from other fruits (apple, pear, cranberry, peach), as well as five different hard ciders. Their sparkling dry ciders are delicious. You can taste all of these for a small fee in the wine barn, built in the 1850s as a tool shed, and which housed the cider press from the 1950s to 1990s.

Hopkins Vineyard, 25 Hopkins Rd., Warren 06777; (860) 868-7954; hopkins vineyard.com. Check the website for opening hours. Once a dairy farm located on Lake Waramaug, this property was transformed by its owners, Bill and Judith Hopkins, into one of Connecticut's first vineyards in 1979. They grow 11 varieties of grapes on the property, including Chardonnay, Cabernet Franc, Vidal Blanc, Dornfelder, Lemberger, Pinot Noir, and Cayuga White. They make red, white, and sparkling wines, as well as apple and peach wine. This property, which has been owned by the Hopkins family for more than 200 years, has views of the lake from the wine bar in the hayloft of their barn, which makes it a perfect place to enjoy some wine. Wine can be purchased by the glass or bottle along with cheese, bread, and pâté. There are two other bars at which to taste wine in the barn. When the weather is warm, take your wine outside—the property is great for a walk and there are plenty of tables and chairs out in the fresh air. For a fee, they offer a guided tour, which includes a walk through the vines, the winery, and the cellar. They have a very well-stocked gift shop if you are looking for a present for a wine lover. The perfect gift, however, would be a bottle of their ice wine, a rare treat to find made by a Connecticut producer.

Jerram Winery, 535 Town Hill Rd. (Route 219), New Hartford 06057; (860) 379-8749; jerramwinery.com. Open May 1 through Dec 31, Fri through Sat, 11 a.m. to 5 p.m. Check the website for winter hours. Closed for the month of April. Jim Jerram produces about 1,000 cases of wine a year from the grapes he grows on his 10 acres in the historic Town Hill section of New Hartford, the part of town first settled in the early 1700s. He began growing grapes and making wine as a hobby, which evolved into this business in 1998, in a converted horse barn. It's a lovely property with an elevation of 1,000 feet, which means the grapes are picked a little later, as at that height they have a longer growing season. He grows Marechal Foch, Chambourcin, Seyval Blanc, Chardonnay, Villard Bland, Vignoles, and St. Croix grapes and makes 11 wines, both red and white; he also produces a rosé wine. The tasting room is located in a converted arts-and-crafts-style building dating from 1904 that once served as a creamery on the property and was used for making butter. With places to sit and enjoy a picnic lunch and a glass or two of wine—on the patio, in the gardens planted with lilies, or among the vines—it's a lovely spot to visit on a sunny day when the weather is warm. There's a fee for the tasting. When you visit, ask for a tour, and your wish may be granted.

Jonathan Edwards Winery, 74 Chester Main Rd., North Stonington 06359; (860) 535-0202; jedwardswinery.com. Open Sun through Fri, 11 a.m. to 5 p.m.; Sat, 11 to 4:30 p.m. (last tasting at 4 p.m.). Tours offered at noon. It's an unusual twist when a New England family goes to Napa Valley, makes a success of winemaking, and then returns to their roots in New England to begin winemaking on the East Coast while still running the West Coast vineyard. Jonathan Edwards and his parents, Bob and Karen, bought an existing 48-acre vineyard, the Crosswoods Vineyard, in 2000, planted 20 acres of vines, and began making wine on both coasts. A very good thing for Nutmeggers it is, too, as they make top-quality wines, perhaps the best in the state. The property the Edwards family purchased was first owned by the

Williams family in the 1700s, based on information found on old maps, and in the 20th century it was used as a dairy farm run by the Maine family. Today it is a place to go to not only taste their excellent wines, but as a focus of art shows for local artists, charity events, road races, weddings, and other events in a very beautiful setting among their vines. If you visit, it's important to call ahead, particularly on the weekend, as parking is limited and the place is always buzzing when the weather is bright and sunny.

Land of Nod Winery, 99 Lower Rd., East Canaan 06024; (860) 824-5225; landofnodwinery.com. Open Sat and Sun, 11 a.m. to 5 p.m., Apr and May and Sept through mid-Nov. From June through Aug. they are open Fri, Sat, and Sun, 11 a.m. to 5 p.m. In April and May, they open on Fri, 11 a.m. to 5 p.m., but for purchase only, no tours. Owned by the Adam family, this small family-run winery, located on a 200-acre farm dating back to the American Revolution in the foothills of the Berkshires, beneath Canaan Mountain and near the Blackberry River, is a bit off the beaten path. But it's a gorgeous ride among rolling hills deep into the country to get there, and the winery is an attractive place to spend an hour or two. The family planted the first vines in 1994 and William P. Adam began to make wine in 1998. The range of grape wines—Bianca, Rosé, Corot Noir, Marquette, Ironmaster Reserve (the name is a reference to Beckley Furnace, Connecticut's best preserved iron works from the 19th century on the river, where the falls nearby are a great place to cool off on a hot day)—join with peach, raspberry, and blueberry wines (and another that combines the two berries). But the list often changes and evolves. They also sell the wool from their herd of Corriedale sheep if you'd like to knit a sweater, handmade wreaths, and fresh farm eggs. From February to April each year they offer tours of their sugarhouse, selling the maple products alongside the wine in their shop. Self-guided tours of the property are encouraged, as is picnicking—which you won't be able to resist once you see this pretty place, so plan ahead and bring some lunch.

McLaughlin Vineyards, 14 Albert's Hill Rd., Sandy Hook 06482; (203) 426-1533; mclaughlinvineyards.com. Open Wed to Fri, 11 a.m. to 5 p.m.; Sat, 11 a.m. to 5:30 p.m.; Sun, noon to 5:30 p.m. Bruce McLaughlin and his family own this vineyard, which was established in 1979, in a secluded, quiet setting. McLaughlin is the winemaker and Dee Dee Morlock is the manager. The vineyard is comprised of 160 acres set along the Housatonic River. The tasting room and winery can be found in the converted 19th-century barn on the property, surrounded by wooded hills and flower gardens. Try their wines, both red and white, made from Aurore, Chardonnay, Merlot, Foch, Norton, and Vidal Blanc grapes. Plan to visit during warm weather and have a picnic on the lawns or terrace, then take a walk on the hiking trails. Check the website for some unusual events they hold, including a music festival and vintage baseball games held once a month during the warm months.

Miranda Vineyard, 42 Ives Rd., Goshen 06756; (860) 491-9906; mirandavineyard .com. The hours change with the seasons, so check their website before you travel. Located in the Litchfield hills, this winery, with its rocky New England soil and cool breezes that flow down from Mohawk Mountain and across Woodridge Lake, is owned by the Miranda family. Grapes and winemaking are part of Manny Miranda's Portuguese heritage. He began to make wine as a boy with his grandfather and father, and owning a vineyard modeled after his family's business in Europe became his dream. So in 2001, he, his wife, Maria, and their sons planted their first vines, and in 2007, opened their winery. Their business is very much a family affair and, because their grapes and wines are organic, it takes lots of manpower to tend the grapes without the help of chemicals, net the vines to protect them, and harvest by hand. They grow all their grapes, including Chardonnay, Seyval Blanc, Merlot, and Cayuga White, and produce 10 wines including reds, whites, a rosé, and several sweet wines. Drawing on their Portuguese heritage, they produce a white Port and Jerupiga, a traditional Portuguese dessert wine. If you visit, this is a lovely spot from which to watch the sunset over Mohawk Mountain. The family will make you feel at home and you won't want to take your eyes off the view from their deck. Check their website for special events including live music, a harvest festival, and chocolate tastings.

Preston Ridge Vineyard, 100 Miller Rd., Preston 06365; (860) 383-4278; prestonridgevineyard.com. Check the website for opening times. This winery in eastern Connecticut opened in 2012 and is the brainchild of two families—the Sawyers and the Helms—who decided to grow grapes and make wine together in 2008. Among the 60 acres they own, they have six acres of vines and grow Chardonnay, Cabernet Franc, Riesling, Tiraminetter, Vidal Blanc, and Baco Noir in an gorgeous setting on the peak of a ridge, 15 miles away from Long Island Sound. The position of the vineyards benefits from the moderating temperatures and the climate near the water. About 80 percent of their grapes come from New York as their vines are so young. They produce nine wines including reds, whites, and rosé. The views from the tasting room in their gray barn are panoramic, and the space itself is roomy, airy, and full of light. There are plenty of tables and chairs inside as well as on their deck outside, with nice tables made from barrels and where the views are breathtaking. During the summer they have live music on Friday nights and Sunday afternoons. Bring a picnic, buy some wine, and enjoy the gorgeous vista. The enthusiasm of these young owners will inspire you to return for more.

Priam Vineyards, 11 Shailor Hill Rd., Colchester 06415; (860) 267-8520; priamvineyards.com. Open March through Dec, but check the website for days and hours, as they change with the season. Located deep in the woods in the Salmon River Watershed area, this property has been designated a natural bird and wildlife habitat by the National Wildlife Federation, in part because the owners encourage bluebirds to do the work of insecticides to keep their vines healthy. Gloria Priam, business manager, and Brian Crump, enologist, own the 40-acre property with 24 acres of vineyards, and produce 13 wines from the European varietals they grow on the property, including Cabernet Franc, Cabernet Sauvignon, Chardonnay, Gewurztraminer, Merlot, Muscat, and Riesling as well as French-American hybrids, Cayuga and St. Croix. Opened in 2003, the business is named for Priam's grandfather, who had a vineyard in Hungary in the early 1900s. They offer tastings and tours of the vineyard, for which there is a charge. Bring a picnic, buy a bottle of wine, and enjoy it on their patio. Take home a few bottles with names of places located nearby—Salmon River Red or White, Blackledge Rosé, Westchester Red—as a souvenir of your visit. On Fridays, July through August, from 6 to 9 p.m., there's live music on the grounds; check the website for fees.

Rosedale Farms & Vineyard, 25 East Weatogue St., Simsbury 06070; (860) 651-3926; rosedale1920.com. Check the website for months and times when they are open. This family farm, run by Lynn and Marshall Epstein, has been supplying top quality vegetables, fruit, and flowers to the locals since 1920. Recently, in the good hands of their neighbor, Charlie Stephenson, also their vineyard manager and winemaker, they have begun to grow their grapes on 4 of the farm's 120 acres and to make wine. They opened their winery in 2005, and the farm has become a destination for wine lovers and foodies because of the chef-to-table dinners they host. They grow French hybrid grapes—St. Croix, Petite Sirah, Seyval Blanc, Vidal Blanc, Cayuga, and Vignoles—and produce about 1,000 cases per year. Visit the farm store, where they sell their produce (locals say they sell the best sweet corn); stroll the grounds, where the scenery is very pretty; and be sure to taste some wine at the outdoor bar behind the shop. They move tastings inside at the end of the growing season. For a fee (check their website) you not only get a wine tasting with substantial pours, but a free wine glass and a generous plate of cheese, crackers, fruit, and dip. The wines are delicious, so get there early in the season, as they usually sell out.

Saltwater Farm Vineyard, 349 Elm St., Stonington 06378; (860) 415-9072; saltwaterfarmvineyard.com. Check the website for opening times. Housed in a 1930s airplane hangar in a beautiful 100-acre location near the tidal marshes of Wequetequock Creek, and with views of Long Island Sound, this winery, owned by Michael M. Connery, was opened in 2003. The land was first farmed by Walter Palmer, who came to New England from England in 1629, settled in the Massachusetts Bay Colony, and then came to the area and began farming on the Saltwater Farm property in 1653. Herbert West farmed the property until the early 20th century. In the 1930s, a small airport called Foster Field and a hangar were built on the property by William J. Foster. The US government closed the airport, as well as others like

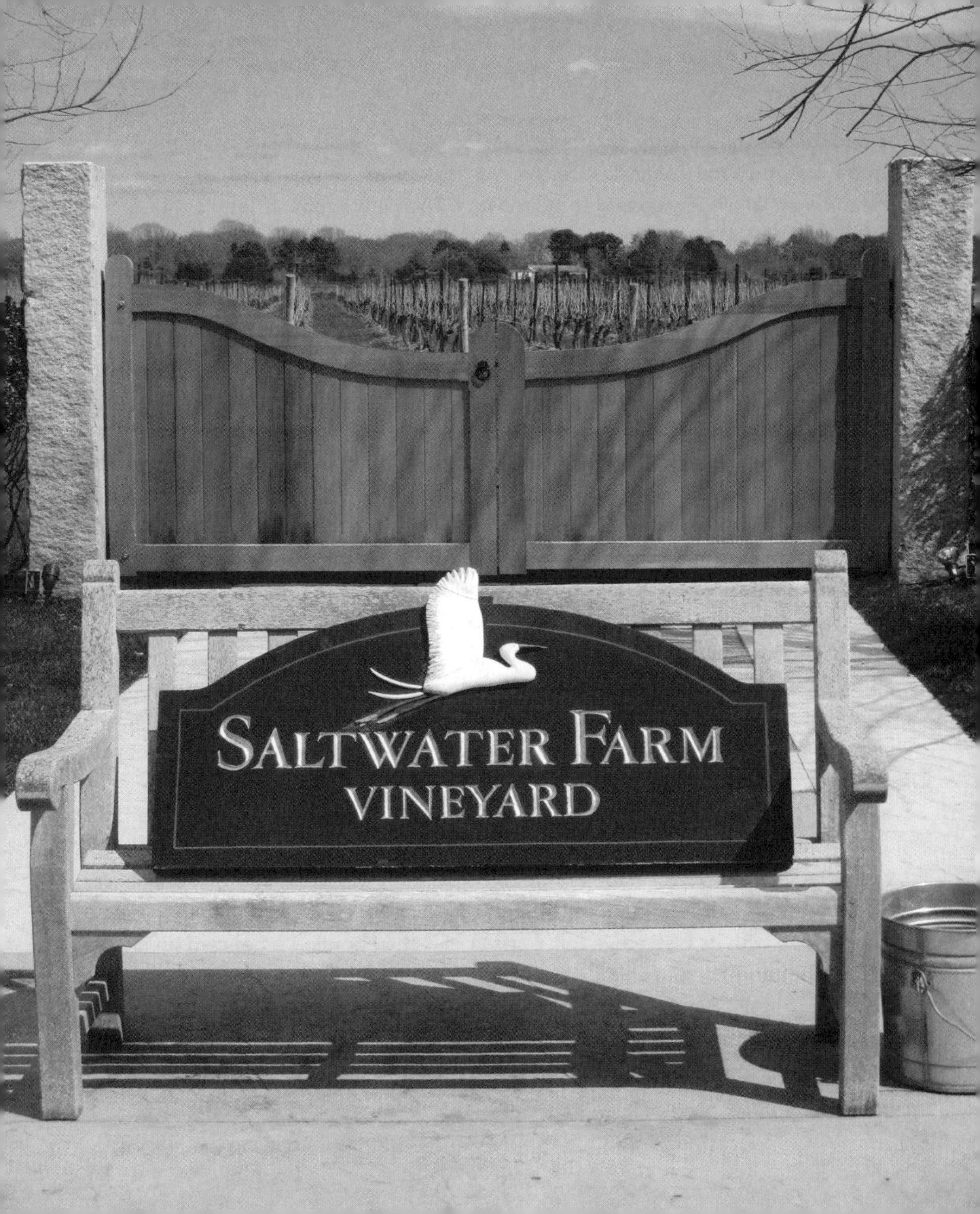
SALTWATER FARM
VINEYARD

it throughout the country, to public use for security reasons just after the United States entered World War II. After the war, the property was used for a few years for commercial air service and to train pilots. Then it was abandoned until Connery purchased it in 2001. Today, in addition to the winery, the property is also a bird sanctuary (you might spot an osprey, and lots of hummingbirds appear on the patio). Because of its location just off US 1 on a road that leads to the charms of Stonington Borough with its restaurants, pretty houses, and antique shops, the tasting room gets very crowded. Parking can be difficult, particularly when traffic control is in the hands of the owner, whose patience often runs thin ("Why doesn't someone else police the parking lot instead of that grumpy man?" is a question you will hear visitors asking again and again). The restored hangar, now incorporating timber trusses and a vaulted roof, looks from the outside like a shiny aluminum spaceship, emphasized by the fact that it appears somewhat out of place as it looms up out of the natural beauty and breathtaking scenery of the marshland and the vines. Fifteen acres are planted with Cabernet Franc, Merlot, Pinot Noir, Chardonnay, Sauvignon Blanc, and Gewurztraminer vines. They have hired a French winemaker to supervise the production of wine and make about 1,500 cases per year. Taste their wines, buy a bottle, and drink it with a picnic lunch on the patio. Then take a walk through the vines that lead to a walk to the sea. It's a lovely way to spend an afternoon. Check the website, as they occasionally offer live music events in this beautiful environment.

Sharpe Hill Vineyard, 108 Wade Rd., Promfret 06258; (860) 974-3549; sharpehill .com. Check the website for opening hours. Owned by Steven and Catherine Vollweiler, this vineyard sits on about 25 acres in the Quiet Corner of Connecticut. Howard Bursen is the winemaker at this vineyard, best known for their Ballet of Angels wine with its distinctive folk portrait of a child holding a pet bird on a string on its label and its refreshing flowery flavor achieved from a blend of about 10 different grapes. Because of the quality of their wine and perhaps the beautiful surroundings, Sharpe Hill has become one of Connecticut's best-loved wineries. Stroll through the vineyards, and when you reach the top of the hill you can see three states on a clear day. They grow Chardonnay, Riesling, Carmine, Cabernet

Franc, St. Croix, and Vignoles grapes on this property and produce about 16,500 cases of wine annually. What is remarkable for a Connecticut winery is that their red wines are excellent; in fact, their Cabernet Franc wine is a superstar. The tasting room, full of antiques and paintings, is quite small, but an interesting place to taste wine. They have a restaurant, Fireside Tavern, opened in the 1990s, that serves excellent food, including vegetables and herbs from their garden, but you should note that you can only dine there if you have made reservations in advance. There are lovely views of the property if you eat inside, but a meal in the wine garden when the weather is good is a memorable experience and a lovely backdrop for drinking some of their delicious wines.

Stonington Vineyards, 523 Taugwonk Rd., Stonington 06378; (860) 535-1222; stoningtonvineyards.com. Open mostly daily, 11 a.m. to 5 p.m., but check website for closing days. In 1989 Nick and Happy Smith started their vineyard on 58 acres of land close to Long Island Sound. The position of the vines close to the sea and the resulting microclimate in which their grapes grow is similar to the conditions for growing grapes that are found in Bordeaux. Today they make 5,000 to 7,000 cases of wine annually, selling most of their wine in their tasting room. Popular locally, wine drinkers often discover the wines they produce on the menus of restaurants along the Connecticut coastline, particularly the Seaport White, named for Mystic Seaport located just down the road a few miles. It is often the house white in restaurants nearby. It's more fun, however, to visit the vineyard and taste the wines where they are produced. They charge a fee for their tastings; check the website for prices. Although the bar is pretty small, there's room for quite a crowd in the tasting room. Their patio is a great place to enjoy some wine on a sunny day. Mike McAndrew is the winemaker, and he's turned out excellent chardonnays as well as blended wines, such as their blended red called Triad Rosé and also wines made from Vidal Blanc, Riesling, and Cabernet Franc grapes. They offer vineyard tours every day at 2 p.m. One of the great annual events they stage is their wine festival held in tents on their lawn, where visitors can not only taste wine, but buy some great food to go with it.

Sunset Meadow Vineyards

Sunset Meadow Vineyards, 599 Old Middle St. (Route 63), Goshen 06756; (860) 201-4654; sunsetmeadowvineyards.com. Open year-round, Mon, Thurs, and Sun, 11 a.m. to 5 p.m.; Fri and Sat, 11 a.m. to 6 p.m. George and Judy Motel own this small farm of 32 acres in the Litchfield Hills, which they purchased in 1996 and originally ran as a beef and hay farm. They made the transition to vineyards and opened their winery in 2007. They chose a gorgeous position facing west, which is not only good for watching sunsets, but also for growing grapes. They may be small, but they make a long list of wines from the grapes they grow—12 at last count—a little unusual among Connecticut winemakers who usually buy some if not most of their grapes from growers in upstate New York, on Long Island, or in California. They are open year-round, another reason they stand out from other producers in the state. It's a nice place to visit to drink a little wine, even in the winter, accompanied by a bit of cheese or salami that you can buy right there, and to keep warm by their pot-bellied stove in the cozy tasting room. Their Vidal Blanc and Twisted Red are delicious wines; you might consider bringing home a bottle of each for everyday drinking. Come back in the warm months, when you can sit on the patio or the lawn and watch that famous sunset with a glass in your hand.

Taylor Brooke Winery, 848 Route 171, Woodstock 06281; (860) 974-1263; taylorbrookewinery.com. Open April 25 through Dec 31, Fri, 11 a.m. to 6 p.m.; Sat and Sun, 11 a.m. to 5 p.m. Located in the beautiful hills of the northeast corner of the state known as "the Quiet Corner," this winery has been in business since 2004. Linda and Richard Auger—he's the winemaker—are the owners of this property with its three acres of vines under cultivation. They produce 15 wines from the grapes they grow on their property and purchase some of their grapes from local farmers. Their most popular wine is the St. Croix Rosé, but they also produce fruit-concentrate-infused (cranberry, green apple, peach, pomegranate, raspberry) Rieslings, popular with those who have a sweeter palate, along with a long list of other wines. The wine labels are designed by Tom Menard, a local artist, who works in a folk art style. The comfortable tasting room is a great place to sample the wines (for a fee, check the site for prices) and they encourage visitors to picnic on the grounds, so bring a picnic or buy the local cheeses, sausages, crackers, and dips they sell. If you like their wines, you can adopt one of their vines, or buy it as a gift for a wine lover. For $55 including tax, you can "own" one of their vines, receive a certificate of adoption, be invited to participate in the harvest, and be allowed to take home one bottle of wine per year for three years (the bottles have to be picked up at the winery). It's such a friendly place, and the Augers and their staff are so enthusiastic that it just seems right to own a little piece of it!

White Silo Farm & Winery, 32 Route 37 East, Sherman 06784; (860) 355-0271; whitesilowinery.com. Open April through Dec, Fri, noon to 8 p.m., Sat and Sun, 11 a.m. to 6 p.m. Purchased in 1990, this family-run farm is located in a beautiful setting with terrific views among the hills south of Litchfield County, and on a piece of property that belonged to the Upland Pastures Dairy Farm. The father-son team of Ralph and Eric Gorman have produced fruit wines since 2010 from the grapes, berries, and rhubarb they grow and also sell. Known for their food festivals, with food to sample and plenty of live music, they mark the start of the growing season celebrating the harvest of their asparagus in May, rhubarb in June, and raspberries in September. They've restored the 18th-century red barn with its distinctive white silo, stone walls, and old beams, and transformed it into their wine-tasting room with a long bar, wooden tables, and chairs for visitors. They produce both dry and semisweet wines from White Cayuga and Red Frontenac grapes, raspberries, blackberries, black currants, and rhubarb. The sparkling raspberry wine and the blackberry sangria they make are very tasty. Check the website for tasting charges. You can bring a picnic or buy a cheese plate there, and if you phone ahead, they will prepare a boxed lunch for you to purchase. Enjoy your meal in one of their pretty terrace gardens with some of their wine. They also make a variety of flavored mustards and jams, all delicious, that you can also purchase. You can also visit and pick your own raspberries and blackberries from August to October.

APPENDIX A:
Travel Planner: List of Producers Organized by Town/City

Bantam

Arethusa Farm Dairy, 822 Bantam Rd., Bantam 06750; (860) 361-6600; arethusafarm.com. Open Tues and Wed, 12 to 7 p.m.; Thurs and Sun, 10 a.m. to 7 p.m.; Fri and Sat, 10 a.m. to 8 p.m. Food: ice cream, milk, cheese, and other dairy products

Bantam Bread Company, 853 Bantam Rd., Bantam 06750; (860) 567-2737; bantambread.com. Open Wed through Sat, 8:30 a.m. to 5:30 p.m.; Sun, 8:30 a.m. to 4 p.m. Food: bread and other types of baked goods

Bantam Tileworks, 816 Bantam Rd., Bantam 06750; (860) 361-9306; bantamtileworks.com. Open Mon through Fri, 9:30 a.m. to 5 p.m.; Sat through Sun, 10 a.m. to 5 p.m. Ceramics/Pottery: stoneware tiles and pottery

Bloomfield

Back East Brewery, 1296A Blue Hills Ave., Bloomfield 06002; (860) 242-1793; backeastbrewing.com. Tastings offered Wed through Fri, 4 to 7 p.m., and Sat, noon to 4 p.m. Beer

Thomas Hooker Brewery, 16 Tobey Rd., Bloomfield 06002; (860) 242-3111; hookerbeer.com. Gift shop and growler filling hours are Mon through Fri, 9 a.m. to 5 p.m.; Sat, noon to 5 p.m. Tastings are held the first and third Friday of every month from 5 to 8 p.m. Beer

Branford

Clay Bodies Pottery, LLC, 59 School Ground Rd., Unit 4, Branford 06405; (203) 488-3772; claybodiespottery.com. Visit by appointment only. Pottery

JC ArtGlass Designs LLC, 59 North Harbor, Branford 06405; (203) 481-0408; jcartglass.com. Visit by appointment only. Glass

Thimble Island Brewing Company, 16 Business Park Dr., Branford; (203) 208-2827; thimbleislandbrewery.com. Tasting room is open Thurs through Fri, 3 to 8 p.m.; Sat, 11 a.m. to 8 p.m.; Sun, noon to 5 p.m. Tours are Sat, noon, 2, and 4 p.m., and Sun, 1 and 3 p.m. Beer

Bridgewater

Stuart Family Farm Stand, 191 Northrup St. (off route 133), Bridgewater 06752; (860) 355-0172; stuartfamilyfarm.com. Open Sat, 10 a.m. to 4 p.m.; Sun, noon to 4 p.m. Food: beef, pork, and chicken

Bristol

Firefly Hollow Brewing Co., 139 Center St., Bristol 06010, (860) 845-8977; fireflyhollowbrewing.com. Open Thurs through Fri, 2 to 8 p.m.; Sat, noon to 8 p.m.; and Sun, noon to 5 p.m. Beer

Brookfield

Bridgewater Chocolate Company, 559 Federal Rd., Brookfield 06804; (203) 775-2286; bridgewaterchocolate.com. Check website for hours of operation. Chocolate

DiGrazia Vineyards, 131 Tower Rd., Brookfield 06804; (203) 775-1616; digrazia .com. Open daily, May through Dec, 11 a.m. to 5 p.m. Call to make an appointment if you'd like to visit at other times. Wine

Simpson & Vail, 3 Quarry Rd., Brookfield 06804; (203) 775-0240; svtea.com. Open year-round Mon through Fri, 9 a.m. to 5:30 p.m. Open Sat, 10 a.m. to 4 p.m., Sept through June. Beverages, non-alcoholic: tea and coffee

Brooklyn

Architectural Stained Glass, 211 Hartford Rd., Brooklyn 06234; (860) 774-7040; asgstudio.com. Visit by appointment only. Glass

Meadow Stone Farm, 199 Hartford Rd., Brooklyn 06234; (860) 617-2982; meadowstonefarm.com. Call or check the website for hours. Closed Jan and Feb. Cheese: goat cheese and goat milk products

Canton

Hickory Ledges Farm & Distillery, 183 Bahre Corner Rd., Canton 06019; (860) 693-4039; hickoryledges.com. Visit by appointment only. Alcoholic spirits

Chester

Dina Varano, 27 Main St., Chester 06412; (860) 526-8866; dinavarano.com. Open Tues through Fri, 11 a.m. to 6 p.m.; Sat, 10 a.m. to 6 p.m.; Sun, 11 a.m. to 5 p.m. Jewelry

Lori Warner Studio/Gallery, 21 Main St., Chester 06412; (860) 322-4265; loriwarner.com. Check website for hours. Prints and paintings

Clinton

Chamard Vineyards, 115 Cow Hill Rd., Clinton 06413; (860) 664-0299; chamard .com. Check the website for opening times. Wine

Colchester

Cato Corner Farm, 178 Cato Corner Rd., Colchester 06415; (860) 537-3884; catocornerfarm.com. Open Fri and Sat, 10 a.m. to 4 p.m.; Sun, 11 a.m. to 4 p.m. Cheese from cow's milk

Priam Vineyards, 11 Shailor Hill Rd., Colchester 06415; (860) 267-8520; priamvineyards.com. Open March through Dec, Wed through Sun. Check the website for hours and tasting fees. Wine

Collinsville

Carol & Company, 107 Main St., Collinsville 06019; (860) 693-1088; carolandcompany.us. Check the website for seasonal hours. Jewelry

Coventry

BeeZ by Scranton, 1804 Boston Tpke., Coventry 06238; (860) 450-9240; beezbyscranton.com. Visit by appointment only. Vintage purses.

East Canaan

Land of Nod Winery, 99 Lower Rd., East Canaan 06024; (860) 824-5225; landofnodwinery.com. Open Sat and Sun, 11 a.m. to 5 p.m., Apr and May and Sept through mid-Nov. From June through Aug they are open Fri, Sat, and Sun, 11 a.m. to 5 p.m. In Apr and May, they open on Fri, 11 a.m. to 5 p.m., but for purchase only, no tours. Wine

Eastford

Buell's Orchard, 108 Crystal Pond Rd., Eastford 06242; (860) 974-1150; buellsorchard.com. Check the website for hours. Wine

Heidi Howard, Maker & Painter, P.O. Box 112, Eastford 06242; (860) 974-3979; heidihoward.com. Visit by appointment only. Folk art signs

East Hartford

Olde Burnside Brewing Company, 776 Tolland St., East Hartford 06108; (860) 528-2200; oldeburnsidebrewing.com. Open Sat, 1 to 4 p.m. Beer

Onyx Moonshine, 64-D Oakland Ave.; East Hartford 06108; (860) 550-1939; onyxmoonshine.com. Visit by appointment only. Alcoholic spirits

East Hartland

Sweet Wind Farm, 339 South Rd., East Hartland 06027, (860) 653-2038; sweetwindfarm.net. Contact the company about opening times. Food: maple syrup and maple sugar products

East Haven

Overshores Brewing Co., 250 East Bradley St., East Haven 06512; overshores .com. Check the website for opening times. Beer

Sugar Bakery, 422-424 Main St., East Haven 06512; (203) 469-0815; thesugarbakery .com. Open Mon through Wed and Sat, 9 a.m. to 5 p.m.; Thurs through Fri, 9 a.m. to 6 p.m. Food: cookies, cakes, and other baked items

East Windsor

Broad Brook Brewing Co., 2 North Rd., East Windsor 06088; (860) 623-1000; broadbrookbrewing.com. Open Wed, 3 to 7 p.m.; Thurs, 3 to 9 p.m.; Fri, 2 to 9 p.m.; Sat, noon to 7 p.m.; Sun, noon to 5 p.m. Beer

Fairfield

Hot Spot Glass Studio, 112 Post Rd., Fairfield 06824; (203) 257-7958; hotspotglass .com. Visit by appointment. Glass

Falls Village

Rustling Winds Stables and Creamery, 148 Canaan Mountain Rd., Falls Village 06031; (860) 824-7084; rustlingwind.com. Open daily from 8:30 a.m. to 4:30 p.m. Cow's milk cheese

Gales Ferry

Holmberg Orchards & Winery, 12 Orchard Lane, Gales Ferry 06335; (860) 464-7305; holmbergwinery.com. Check website for winery and farm market hours. Wine, fruit, and vegetables

Glastonbury

Dee's One Smart Cookie, 398 Hebron Ave., Glastonbury 06033; (860) 633-8000; deesonesmartcookie.com. Open Mon, noon to 5 p.m.; Tues through Fri, 8:30 a.m. to 6 p.m.; Sat, 8:30 a.m. to 3 p.m. Gluten-free, dairy free, tree nut free, peanut free, and soy-free bakery

Fintar Guitars, 122 Naubuc Ave., Nap Brothers Building, Glastonbury 06033; (860) 944-5387. Visits by appointment only. Guitars designed with classic car embellishments

Joseph Preli Farm and Vineyard, 235 Hopewell Rd., South Glastonbury 06073; (860) 633-7333; josephprelifarm.com. Check website for opening times. Fruit, vegetables, herbs, and grapes

Killam & Bassette Farmstead, LLC, 14 Tryon St., South Glastonbury 06073; (860) 833-0095; kandbfarmstead.com. Open 9 a.m. to 6 p.m., year-round. Fruit, vegetables, flowers, pork, chicken, fresh eggs, baked goods, honey, jams, jellies, pickles, fruit sauces, and relishes

Phoenix Welding, 122 Naubuc Ave. (at the rear of the Nap Brothers building), Glastonbury 06033; (860) 657-9481. Visit by appointment only. Metal custom-made chairs, tables, bar rails, metal signs, and fire pits

Rose's Berry Farm, 295 Matson Hill Rd., South Glastonbury 06073; (860) 633-7467; rosesberryfarm.com. Check the website for hours. Fruit, jams, vinegars, salsas, vegetables, pies and other baked goods, and local honey

So. G Coffee Roasters, 882 Main St., South Glastonbury 06073; (860) 633-8500; sogcoffee.com. Open Mon through Fri, 6 a.m. to 4:30 p.m.; Sat, 7 a.m. to 4:30 p.m.; Sun 8 a.m. to 1 p.m. Coffee and tea

Woodland Farm LLC, 575 Woodland St., South Glastonbury 06703; (860) 633-2742; woodlandfarmllc.com. Check website for opening hours. Fruit and apple cider

Goshen

Miranda Vineyard, 42 Ives Rd., Goshen 06756; (860) 491-9906; mirandavineyard .com. The hours change with the seasons, so check their website before you travel. Wine

Nodine's Smokehouse, 39 North St. (Route 63), Goshen 06756; (860) 491-4009; nodinesmokehouse.com. Open Mon through Sat, 9 a.m. to 5 p.m.; Sun 10 a.m. to 4 p.m. Smoked meats, fish, and cheeses

Sunset Meadow Vineyards, 599 Old Middle St. (Route 63), Goshen 06756; (860) 201-4654; sunsetmeadowvineyards.com. Open year-round, Mon, Thurs, and Sun, 11 a.m. to 5 p.m.; Fri and Sat, 11 a.m. to 6 p.m. Wine

Thorncrest Farm and Milk House Chocolates, 280 Town Hill Rd., Goshen; (860) 309-2545; milkhousechocolates.net. Summer hours: Thurs through Sat, 10 a.m. to 5 p.m.; Sun, 10 a.m. to 4 p.m.; winter hours: Fri and Sat, 10 a.m. to 5 p.m.; Sun, 10 a.m. to 4 p.m. Chocolates and milk

Greenwich

Black Forest Pastry Shop, 52 Lewis St., Greenwich 06830; (203) 629-9330; blackforestpastryshop.com. Open Mon through Sat, 7:30 a.m. to 6 p.m.; Sun, 8 a.m. to 1 p.m. Baked goods: pastries, cakes, and other items with a German twist, plus gelato, chocolates, and jams

Guilford

Bishops Orchards Winery and Farm Market, 1355 Boston Post Rd. (Route 1), Guilford 06437; (866) 224-7467; bishopsorchardswinery.com. Open Mon through Sat, 8 a.m. to 7 p.m.; Sun, 9 a.m. to 6 p.m. Wine, baked goods, farm products and groceries

Carol Grave, 1298 Moose Hill Rd., Guilford 06437; (203) 314-8003; carolgrave .com. Visit by appointment only. Woven rugs, wall hangings, quilts, clothing, and accessories

Red Rooster Gourmet Cookies, 16 Church St., Guilford 06437; (203) 533-4220; redroosterbaking.com. Open Tues through Sat, 9 a.m. to 6 p.m.; Sun, 9 a.m. to 3 p.m. Cookies

Hartford

The Brothers Crisp, 1477 Park St., Ste. 2E, Hartford 06106; (860) 385-2040; thebrotherscrisp.com. Open Mon through Fri, 9 a.m. to 5 p.m. Hand-made shoes

DiFiore Ravioli Shop, 556 Franklin Ave., Hartford 06114; (860) 296-1077; difioreraviolishop.com. Open Mon through Fri, 9 a.m. to 6 p.m.; Sat, 9 a.m. to 5 p.m.; Sun 10 a.m. to 4 p.m. Italian sauces, pastas, ravioli, and other prepared foods

Hardenco, 30 Bartholomew Ave., Hartford 06106; (860) 880-0495; hartford denimcompany.com. Open Mon through Fri, 10 a.m. to 5 p.m.; Sat by appointment. Jeans and work wear made by hand

The Hartford Artisans Weaving Center, 40 Woodland St., Hartford 06105; (860) 727-5727; weavingcenter.org. Boutique open Mon through Thu, 10 a.m. to 4 p.m. Hand-woven goods, including scarves, shawls, placemats, blankets, wall hangings, and other items

Hartford Prints!, 42 Pratt St., Hartford 06103; (860) 578-8447; hartfordprints.com. Open Tues through Sat, 11 a.m. to 7 p.m. Connecticut-themed cards, notebooks, and T-shirts, invitations, and other printed items

Higganum

CityBench, 73 Maple Ave., Higganum 06441; (860) 716-8111; city-bench.com. Visit by appointment only. Furniture made by hand

Lebanon

Beltane Farm & Tasting House, 59 Taylor Bridge Rd., Lebanon 06249; (860) 887-4709; beltanefarm.com. Check the website for tasting and visiting hours. Goat cheese, raw goat milk, ricotta, and yogurt

Litchfield

Haight-Brown Vineyards, 29 Chestnut Hill Rd., Litchfield 06759; (860) 567-4045; haightvineyards.com. Check the website for opening times. Wine

The Dutch Epicure Shop, 491 Bantam Rd., Litchfield 06759; (860) 567-5586; alldutchfood.com. Open Wed through Sat, 9 a.m. to 5 p.m.; Sun, 9 a.m. to 2 p.m. Baked goods, gourmet food, specializing in Dutch foods

Troy Brook Visions, 38 Clark Rd., Litchfield 06759; (860) 567-2310; troybrookvisions.com. Visit by appointment only. Handcrafted furniture

Lyme

Sankow's Beaver Brook Farm, 139 Beaver Brook Rd., Lyme, CT 06371; (860) 434-2843; beaverbrookfarm.com. Open daily, 9 a.m. to 4 p.m. Farm fresh sheep and cow's milk cheeses

Manchester

Divine Treasures, 404 Middle Tpke. West, Manchester 06040; (860) 643-2552; dtchocolates.com. Open Sun through Tues, 11 a.m. to 6 p.m.; Wed through Thurs, 11 a.m. to 7 p.m.; Fri and Sat, 10 a.m. to 7 p.m. Chocolates and vegan cakes, cheese, ice cream, and other treats

The Spicemill, 191 Adams St., Manchester 06042; (888) 827-8985; espicemill.com. Open Mon through Fri, 9 a.m. to 5 p.m.; Sat, 10 a.m. to 3 p.m. Spices, seasonings, herbs, hot sauces, and cooking oils

Meriden

High Hill Orchard, 170 Fleming Rd., Meriden 06450; (203) 294-0276; highhillorchard.com. Check website for opening hours. Vegetables, fruit, flowers, and herbs is evident

Middlefield

Lyman Orchards, Apple Barrel Market, 32 Reeds Gap Rd., Middlefield 06455; (860) 349-1793; lymanorchards.com. Open daily, 9 a.m. to 6 p.m. Pies made by hand, fruit, vegetables, apple cider, specialty foods, and groceries

Middletown

Tschudin Chocolates & Confections, 100 Riverview Center (at the corner of Main and Court Streets), Middletown 06457; (860) 759-2222; tschocolates.com. Open Thurs, 11 a.m. to 8 p.m.; Fri and Sat, 11 a.m. to 10 p.m.; Sun 11:30 a.m. to 8 p.m. Chocolates

Wesleyan Potters, 350 South Main St., Middletown 06457; (860) 344-0039, wesleyanpotters.com. Open Wed through Sat, 10 a.m. to 5 p.m.; Sun, noon to 4 p.m. Pottery, woven textiles, wooden toys, cutting boards, Christmas decorations, and jewelry

Mystic

Mystic Knotwork, 25 Cottrell St., Mystic 06355; (860) 889-3793; mysticknotwork .com. Open Mon through Thurs and Sat, 10 a.m. to 5 p.m.; Fri, 10 a.m. to 7 p.m. Knotwork bracelets and other decorative items with a nautical twist

New Britain

Avery's, 520 Corbin Ave., New Britain 06052; (860) 224-0830; averysoda.com. Open Tues through Wed, 8:30 a.m. to 5:30 p.m.; Thurs, 8:30 a.m. to 7 p.m.; Fri, 8:30 a.m. to 6 p.m.; Sat, 8:30 a.m. to 3 p.m. Soda

Martin Rosol's, 45 Grove St., New Britain; (860) 223-2707; martinrosolsinc.com. Open Mon and Sat, 8 a.m. to noon; Tues and Wed, 8 a.m. to 2 p.m.; Thurs and Fri, 8 a.m. to 4 p.m. Kielbasa, hot dogs, and other meat products

New Hartford

Connecticut Valley Winery, 1480 Litchfield Tpke. (Route 202), New Hartford 06057; (860) 489-9463; ctvalleywinery.com. Check website for hours. Wine

Jerram Winery, 535 Town Hill Rd. (Route 219), New Hartford 06057; (860) 379-8749; jerramwinery.com. Check website for opening times. Wine

New Haven

Chairigami, 55 Whitney Ave., New Haven 06510; chairigami.com. Open Mon through Fri, 10:30 a.m. to 6 p.m. Cardboard furniture

Newington

Eddy Farm, 851 Willard Ave., Newington 06111; (401) 932-2912; eddyfarmct .com. Open July through Oct; Mon through Fri, 10 a.m. to 6 p.m. (5 p.m. in the fall); Sat and Sun, 10 a.m. to 5 p.m. Vegetables and flowers

Newtown

Folk Art Santas, 165 Hanover Rd., Newtown 06470; (203) 426-2927; folkartsantas .com. Visit by appointment only; check the website for times for their open house. Carved and painted Santa Claus figures

Norfolk

John Garret Thew, Norfolk 06058; (860) 542-5003; email: jthew@att.net. Visits by appointment only. Hand-hammered copper weather vanes

Madeline Falk Fine Art Paintings, Norfolk 06058; (860) 542-6929; madelinefalk .wordpress.com. Visits by appointment only. Dog portraits

Ruthann Olsson, Interior Arts & Design, PO Box 257, 20 John J. Curtis Rd., Norfolk 06058; (860) 542-5095; ruthannolssoninteriors.com. Visit by appointment only. Painted interiors, including hand-painted architectural tromp l'oeuil bordering

North Granby

Sweet Pea Cheese and The House of Hayes Farm, 151 East St.; North Granby 06060; (860) 653-4157; sweetpeacheese.com. Cheese shop is open 10 a.m. to 7 p.m. daily. Dairy products including fresh chèvre, feta, cow and goat milk, chocolate milk, Greek-style goat milk yogurt, whole cow milk yogurt, and scented soaps made from goat milk

North Stonington

Jonathan Edwards Winery, 74 Chester Main Rd., North Stonington 06359; (860) 535-0202; jedwardswinery.com. Open Sun through Fri, 11 a.m. to 5 p.m.; Sat, 11 to 4:30 p.m. (last tasting at 4 p.m.). Tours offered at noon. Wine

Norwalk

Michele's Pies, 666 Main Ave., Norwalk 06851; (203) 354-7144; michelespies.com. Open Tues through Sat, 9 a.m. to 6:30 p.m.; Sun, 10 a.m. to 3 p.m. Pies and other baked goods

Tucci Lumber Bat Co., 227 Wilson Ave., Norwalk 06854; (888) 810-2287; tlbats .com. Visit by appointment only. Baseball bats

Wave Hill Breads/Front Door Bakery, 30 High St., Norwalk 06851; (203) 762-9595; wavehillbreads.com. Open Sat, 10 a.m. to 2 p.m. or pick up orders on Wed until 1 p.m. at the back entrance. Handmade, French country-style bread and other baked products

Oakville

Get Back, Inc., 27 Main St., 4th floor, Oakville 06779; (860) 274-9991; getbackinc .com. Visit by appointment. Original furniture designs and restored vintage American industrial furnishings

Old Lyme

Four Mile River Farm, 124 Four Mile River Rd., Old Lyme 06371; (860) 434-2378; fourmileriverfarm.com. Open daily, 8 a.m. to 6 p.m. Fresh beef, pork, eggs, smoked meats, hooked rugs, and prepared food

Studio 80 + Sculpture Grounds, 80-1 Lyme St., Old Lyme 06371; (860) 434-5957; sculpturegrounds.com and gilbertboro.com. Visit by appointment only. Sculpture

Vasiloff Stained Glass Studio, 4-1 Craig Rd., Old Lyme 06371; (860) 434-9770; vasiloffstainedglass.com. Visit by appointment only. Glass

Old Saybrook

Dagmar's Desserts and Café, 247 Main St., Old Saybrook 06475; (860) 661-4661; dagmarsdesserts.com. Open Tues through Fri, 8:30 a.m. to 5:30 p.m.; Sat, 8 a.m. to 5 p.m.; Sun, 8 a.m. to 1 p.m. German and Austrian baked goods

Hay House Farm, 155 Ingham Hill Rd., Old Saybrook 06475; (860) 575-2387; hayhouseonline.blogspot.com. Farm stand open Thurs, 2:30 to 6 p.m. Flowers, vegetables, jams, jellies, and eggs and paintings

Orange

PEZ Candy Inc, USA, 35 Prindle Hill Rd., Orange 06477-3616; (203) 795-0531; pez.com. Check the website, as hours are seasonal and subject to change at any time. Admission: children under 3 free; children over 3 and adults $4; admission includes a $2 credit for merchandise in the store that day. PEZ candy and dispensers

Oxford

Embracing the Earth, 52 Tram Dr., Oxford; (203) 446-7864; embracingtheearth .com. Visit by appointment only. Pottery and glass could serve as a unique handmade gift for someone special

Pawcatuck

Cottrell Brewing Company, 100 Mechanic St., Pawcatuck 06379; (860) 599-8213; cottrellbrewing.com. Open Fri, 3 to 6 p.m.; Sat, 1 to 6 p.m. Beer

Plainville

Relic Brewing Co., 95 Whiting St., Plainville 06062; (860) 255-4252; relicbeer .com. Open Thurs and Fri, 4 to 7 p.m.; Sat, noon to 4 p.m. Beer

Pomfret

Sharpe Hill Vineyard, 108 Wade Rd., Promfret 06258; (860) 974-3549; sharpehill .com. Check the website for opening hours. Wine and restaurant for fine dining

Preston

Preston Ridge Vineyard, 100 Miller Rd., Preston 06365; (860) 383-4278; prestonridgevineyard.com. Wine

Prospect

Big Dipper Ice Cream Factory, 91 Waterbury Rd., Prospect 06712; (203) 758-3200; bigdipper.com. Check website for hours. Ice cream

Ridgefield

Swoon Bakery, 109 Danbury Rd., The Market Place at Copps Hill Commons, Ridgefield 06877; (203) 438-4326; swoonglutenfree.com. Open Tues through Sat, 10 a.m. to 5 p.m. Gluten- and nut-free bakery

Riverton

Peter Greenwood Glass Blowing Studio, 3 Robertsville Rd., Riverton 06065; (860) 738-9464; petergreenwood.com. Visit by appointment Tues through Sat. Admission is $25 per person, and no more than 10 people are allowed per visit. Glass

Salem

Kismet Letterpress, 123 Music Vale Rd., Salem 06420; (860) 639-6598; kismetletterpress.com. Visit by appointment only. Wedding stationery; invitations; business, note, and holiday cards

Sandy Hook

McLaughlin Vineyards, 14 Albert's Hill Rd., Sandy Hook 06482; (203) 426-1533; mclaughlinvineyards.com. Open Wed through Fri, 11 a.m. to 5 p.m.; Sat, 11 a.m. to 5:30 p.m.; Sun, noon to 5:30 p.m. Wine

Shelton

Jones Family Farms and Jones Winery, 606 Walnut Tree Hill Rd., Shelton 06484; (203) 929-8425; jonesfamily farms.com. See website for seasonal opening hours. Wine, Christmas, harvest-your-own strawberries and blueberries

Sherman

White Silo Farm & Winery, 32 Route 37 East, Sherman 06784; (860) 355-0271; whitesilowinery.com. Open April through Dec, Fri, noon to 8 p.m., Sat and Sun, 11 a.m. to 6 p.m. Wine, fruit, vegetables, mustards, and jams

Simsbury

Rosedale Farms & Vineyard, 25 East Weatogue St., Simsbury 06070; (860) 651-3926; rosedale1920.com. Check the website for months and times they are open. Wine, vegetables, fruit, and flowers

Southington

Rogers Orchard, 336 Long Bottom Rd., Southington 06489, (860) 229-4240; rogersorchards.com. Check website for opening hours. Fruit, cider, vegetables, and baked goods

South Norwalk

Elizabeth Eakins Inc., 5 Taft St., South Norwalk 06854; (203) 831-9347; elizabetheakins.com. Call for opening hours. Hand woven rugs and fabrics

South Windsor

Greenleaf Pottery, 240 Chapel Rd., South Windsor 06074; (860) 528-6090; greenleafpottery.net. Open Mon and Wed, 10 a.m. to 5 p.m.; Tue and Thu, 10 a.m. to 9 p.m.; Fri, 10 a.m. to 7 p.m.; Sat, 10 a.m. to 2 p.m. Functional stoneware pottery for the kitchen or table

Stamford

Half Full Brewery, 43 Homestead Ave., Stamford 06902; (203) 658-3631; halfullbrewer.com. Open for tastings Fri, 4 to 7pm; Sat and Sun, noon to 5 p.m. Beer

Stonington

Beer'd Brewing Co., American Velvet Factory, 22 Bayview Ave., Unit 15, Stonington 06355; (860) 857-1014; beerdbrewing.com. Open Fri, 5 to 9 p.m.; Sat and Sun, 1 to 5 p.m. Beer

Cheese Boro Whey, American Velvet Factory, 22 Bayview Ave., Unit 47, Stonington 06378; (860) 235-9654; cheeseborowhey.com. Call for opening times. Ricotta, mozzarella, feta, quark, farm cheese

Saltwater Farm Vineyard, 349 Elm St., Stonington 06378; (860) 415-9072; saltwater farmvineyard.com. Check the website for opening times. Wine

Stonington Seafood Harvester, Stonington Town Dock, 4 High St., Stonington 06378; (860) 535-8342; open 24/7. Flash frozen Bomster scallops, fish, and shrimp

Stonington Vineyards, 523 Taugwonk Rd., Stonington 06378; (860) 535-1222; stoningtonvineyards.com. Open almost daily, 11 a.m. to 5 p.m. (call ahead). Wine

Studio Jeffrey P'an, American Velvet Factory, 22 Bayview Ave., Stonington 06355; (860) 536-9274; studiojeffreypan.com. Open Tues through Sat, 10 a.m. to 5 p.m.; Sun, 11 a.m. to 4 p.m. Glass vessels, sculpture, windows, lighting, and glass and silver jewelry

Zuckermann Harpsichords International, 65 Cutler St., Stonington 06378; (860) 535-1715; zhi.net. Visit by appointment only. Harpsichords and build-it-yourself harpsichord kits

Storrs

UConn Dairy Bar, 3636 Horsebarn Hill Rd. Ext, Storrs 06269; (860) 486-1021; dairybar.uconn.edu. Check the website for opening times, which change throughout the year. Ice cream, milk, cheese, eggs, and many other dairy products

Stratford

Two Roads Brewing Co., 1700 Stratford Ave., Stratford; (203) 335-2010; tworoadsbrewing.com. Open Tues through Sat, noon to 9 p.m.; Sun, noon to 7 p.m. Beer

Southbury

Respond If You Please, 134 Main St. South, Bennett Square, Ste. 68F, Southbury; (203) 217-8737; respondifyouplease.com. Open Tue through Thurs, and Sat, 11 a.m. to 3 p.m. Invitations, stationery, cards, and other printed paper items

Wallingford

Gouveia Vineyards, 1339 Whirlwind Hill Rd., Wallingford 06492; gouveiavineyards .com. Check website for seasonal opening hours. Wine

Warren

Hopkins Vineyard, 25 Hopkins Rd., Warren 06777; (860) 868-7954; hopkinsvineyard .com. Check the website for opening hours. Wine

Waterbury

Sweet Maria's, 159 Manor Ave., Waterbury 06705; (203) 755-3804; sweet-marias .com. Open Tues through Fri, 10 a.m. to 6 p.m.; Sat, 8 a.m. to 6 p.m.; Sun 8 a.m. to noon. Cookies cakes, and cupcakes

Watertown

Reworx Collective, 30 Echo Lake Rd., Watertown, CT 06795; (860) 417-2858; reworxct.com. Visit by appointment only. Furniture, art, lighting, room interiors produced from old materials and found objects

Southwind Farms, 223 Morris Town Line Rd., Watertown 06795; (860) 274-9001; southwindfarms.com. Call for tour and shop hours. Alpaca products, such as yarn, clothing, teddy bears, and many other items

Westbrook

Beach House Glass Beads, 4 Hill St., Westbrook 06498; (860) 339-5098; beachhouseglassbeads.com. Visit by appointment only. Stained glass, lamps, windows, and panels and lamp work beads and jewelry

West Cornwall

Cornwall Bridge Pottery Store, 415 Sharon Goshen Tpke. (Route 128 at the covered bridge), West Cornwall 06796; (860) 672-6545; cbpots.com. Open Sat and Sun, 11 a.m. to 5 p.m. Pottery, including lamps, tableware, serving items, and garden pots, and furniture.

West Granby

The Garlic Farm, 76 Simsbury Rd., West Granby 06090; (860) 264-5644; GarlicFarmCT.com. Open daily, 4th of July through "sometime in Oct," 10 a.m. to 6 p.m. Garlic, vegetables, herbs, and flowers

West Hartford

D. Wilson Art Pottery & Design, West Hartford 06105; (860) 778-1850; dwilsonart.com. Visit by appointment only. Pottery for the kitchen and table

Weston

Red Bee Honey Apiary and Gardens, 77 Lyons Plain Rd., Weston 06883; (203) 226-4535; redbee.com. Visit by appointment only. Honey, beeswax candles, bee pollen, soaps, and skin care products

Westport

Faye Kim Designs, 190 Main St., Westport; (203) 226-3511; fayekimdesigns.com. Open Tues through Sat, 10 a.m. to 5:30 p.m. Jewelry

Saugatuck Craft Butchery, 580 Riverside Ave., Westport 06880; (203) 226-6328; craftbutchery.com. Open Mon through Sat, 10 a.m. to 7 p.m.; Sun, 10 a.m. to 5 p.m. Old-fashioned butcher selling beef, lamb, pork, and poultry

Wethersfield

Carmela's Pasta Shop, 338 Silas Deane Highway, Wethersfield 06109; (860) 529-9533; carmelaspastashop.com. Open Mon through Sat, 9 a.m. to 5 p.m. Fresh pasta, sauces, and Italian dishes

Comstock Ferre & Co, 263 Main St., Wethersfield 06109; (860) 571-6590; rareseeds.com/get-to-know-baker-creek/comstock-ferre. Check website for opening times. Heirloom garden seeds and antiques, gifts including handmade soaps and skincare products, scented candles, fruit preserves and sauces, jewelry, pottery, clothing, household items, stationery, prints and photos

Willimantic

Hosmer Mountain Soda, 217 Mountain St., Willimantic 06226; (860) 423-1555 and 15 Spencer St., Manchester 06040; (860) 643-6923; hosmersoda.com. Open in Willimantic Mon through Sat, 9 a.m. to 6 p.m. Open in Manchester during summer Tues, Wed, Fri, and Sat, 10:30 a.m. to 6 p.m.; and Thurs, 10 a.m. to 9 p.m.. Winter hours in Manchester are Tues, Wed, Fri, and Sat, noon to 6 p.m.; and Thurs, noon to 9 p.m. Soda

Willimantic Brewing Co., 967 Main St., Willimantic 06226; (860) 423-6777; willimanticbrewingcompany.com. Open Mon, 4 p.m. to 1 a.m.; Tue through Thurs, and Sun, 11:30 a.m. to 1 a.m.; and Fri and Sat, 11:30 a.m. to 2 a.m. Beer with brewery and restaurant set up in a 1910 granite and limestone U.S. Post Office Building

Wilton

Nod Hill Soap, 81 Old Ridgefield Rd., Wilton; (203) 210-5347; nodhillsoap.com. Open Tues through Fri, 10:30 a.m. to 3:30 p.m.; Sat, 10:30 a.m. to 2:30 p.m. Soap, body lotions, facial scrubs, lip butters, bath salts, face toners, room sprays, and sachets to scent drawers

Wolcott

Shebeen Brewing Company, 1 Wolcott Rd., Wolcott 06716; (203) 514-2336; shebeenbrewing.com. Open Thurs through Fri, 5 to 9 p.m.; Sat, noon to 7p.m.; Sun, noon to 5 p.m. Beer

Woodbridge

New England Brewing Co., 175 Amity Rd., Woodbridge 06525; (203) 387-2222; newenglandbrewing.com. Open Wed through Fri, 3 p.m. to 7 p.m.; Sat, 11 a.m. to 4 p.m. Beer

Woodbury

James Redway Furniture Makers/The Silver Cherry, 87 Main St. North, Woodbury 06798; (888) 889-2723; redway.com. Open Sat, 10 a.m. to 5 p.m. Eighteenth-century American country-style and nineteenth-century Shaker cherry furniture

Jeffrey Greene Metal Designs, 32 Church St., Woodbury 06798, jeffreygreenemetaldesigns.com. Visit by appointment only. Metal weathervanes, lighting fixtures, art, and useful objects for the home and garden from found metal

Woodbury Pewter, 860 Main St. South, Woodbury 06798; (203) 263-2668. Call to verify opening days and times. Reproduction early American objects in pewter as well as money clips, napkin rings, cork screws, dinnerware, drink stoppers, bowls and bells, tea and coffee pots, pitchers, vases, and porringers, trophies, awards, or commemorative items

Woodstock

Shell Cottage Gallery, Lynda Susan Hennigan, 1089 Route 169, Woodstock 06281; (860) 315-5334; lyndasusanhennigan.com. Open most weekends, but phone for precise times. Sailor's valentines made of shells

Taylor Brooke Winery, 848 Route 171, Woodstock 06281; (860) 974-1263; taylorbrookewinery.com. Open April 25 through Dec 31, Fri, 11 a.m. to 6 p.m.; Sat and Sun, 11 a.m. to 5 p.m. Wine

Appendix B:
Other Places to Buy
Connecticut-Made Products

There are art galleries, boutiques cooperatives, local stores, entire buildings full of creative small businesses (the Velvet Factory in Stonington; several old mills and factories in Parkville in Hartford and in or near Waterbury; the old part of town in Collinsville; the Nap Brothers Building in Glastonbury, and many others in post-industrial landscape of the towns and cities in Connecticut) run by craftsmen, artists, and small businesses. These are just a selection of some of the best supporters of Connecticut-made products:

Ally Bally Bee, 45 Ethan Allen Hwy., Ridgefield 06877; (203) 493-5037; ally-bally-bee.com. Open Mon through Sat, 10 a.m. to 6 p.m.; Sun, noon to 4 p.m. Many products made by Connecticut artists.

Art & Soul, 645 Poquonock Ave. #L, Windsor 06095; (860) 688-4333; artandsoulct .com. Call for opening times. Highlights the work of local artists and craftspeople including glass, pottery, scarves, jewelry, and much more.

Artisans' Marketplace, 120 East St. (Route 10), Plainville 06062; (860) 747-4121; artisansmarketplacect.com. Open Mon through Fri, 10 a.m. to 6 p.m.; Thurs, 10 a.m. to 7 p.m.; Sat, 10 a.m. to 5 p.m.; Sun, 11 a.m. to 4 p.m. Features American-made crafts, including those of a handful of Connecticut artists.

Back 40 Mercantile, 264 Sound Beach Ave., Old Greenwich 06870; (203) 637-0240; back40mercantile.com. Call for opening days and hours. High quality products sourced from small batch purveyors of food products, household goods, furnishings, clothing, and many other things, with many made in Connecticut.

Brookfield Craft Center, 286 Whisconier Rd., Brookfield 06804; (203) 775-4526; brookfieldcraft.org. Call for opening days and hours. Some of the best work Connecticut craftspeople make can be found in the shop.

Caseus Fromagerie & Bistro, 93 Whitney Ave., New Haven; (203) 624-3373; caseusnewhaven.com. Open Mon and Tues, 10:30 a.m. to 5 p.m.; Wed through Sat, 10:30 a.m. to 6 p.m. Cheese shop and bistro selling many Connecticut-produced cheeses including those from Beltane Farm, Cato Corner Farm, Mystic Cheese Co., Arethusa Farm, and Butterfield Farm Company.

Chester Gallery, 76 Main St., Chester; (860) 526-9822. Open Tues through Sat, 10 a.m. to 5 p.m. Connecticut artists' work is displayed.

Colors of the Wind, 360 Main St., Durham 06422; (860) 788-2514; colorsofthe windofdurhamct.com. Known for handmade American products, including those from Connecticut.

The Company of Craftsmen, 43 West Main St., Mystic 06340; (860) 536-4189; companyofcraftsmen.com. Open Mon through Sat, 10 a.m. to 6 p.m.; Sun, 11 a.m. to 6 p.m. Contemporary American crafts.

The Connecticut Store run by the Howland-Hughes Company, Bank Street, Waterbury; (800) 474-6728; ctstore.com. Open Mon through Fri, 10 a.m. to 3 p.m. Sells products made only by Connecticut businesses.

Fine Line Art Gallery, 319 Main St. South, Woodbury 06798; (203) 266-0110; finelineartgallery-connecticut.com. Call for opening hours. A gallery run by a collective of Connecticut artists and craftspeople.

Florence Griswold Museum Shop, 96 Lyme St., Old Lyme 06371; (860) 434-5542; florencegriswoldmuseum.org. Open Tues through Sat, 10 a.m. to 5 p.m.; Sun, 1 to 5 p.m.; closed holidays. Art and handcrafted items produced by Connecticut artists.

Gallery 53, 53 Colony St., Meriden 06451; (203) 235-5347; gallery53.org. Open Tues through Fri, noon to 4 p.m.; Sat, 10 a.m. to 2 p.m. Home of the non-profit The Arts and Crafts Association, its studios, gallery, and shop.

The Gift Shop, Silvermine Galleries, 1037 Silvermine Rd., New Canaan, 06840; (203) 966-9700; silvermineart.org. Open Wed through Sat, noon to 5 p.m.; Sun, 1 to 5 p.m. Work by Connecticut artists and craftspeople.

Guilded Lynx, 458 Main St., Ridgefield 06877; (203) 431-2400; guildedlynx.com. Open Wed through Sat, 10 a.m. to 4 p.m.; Sun, noon to 4 p.m. Jewelry studio, school, gallery.

The Jewelry Cafe, 220 Main St. South, Southbury 06488; (203) 262-8599; thejewelrycafe.com. Open Mon, 10 a.m. to 3 p.m., Tues through Fri, 10:30 a.m. to 6 p.m.; Sat, 10 a.m. to 5 p.m. Jewelry, handbags, clothing, and household accessories made by American artists, many of them from Connecticut.

Lady Bug Boutique, 122 College St., Middletown 06457; (860) 704-6266; ladybug boutique.net. Open Tues, Wed, and Sat, 10 a.m. to 4 p.m.; Thurs, 10 a.m. to 5 p.m.; Fri, 10 a.m. to 6 p.m. Sells Connecticut-produced products and those made in the USA.

Shoppes at Sawmill, 306 Route 169, South Woodstock 06267; (860) 928-7600. Open Mon through Fri, 9 a.m. to 5 p.m.; Sat, 10 a.m. to 5 p.m.; Sun, 11 a.m. to 5 p.m. Local cottage-industry artists, craftspeople, and producers selling food products, paintings, jewelry, and other items.

Small Potatoes Crafts and Gifts, 309 Otrobando Ave., Norwich; (860) 505-9957; smallpotatoescraftsandgifts.com. Open Tues through Fri, 10 a.m. to 5 p.m.; Sat, 10 a.m. to 4 p.m. Arts and crafts produced by local artists.

Swift Waters Cooperative Gallery, 866 Main St., Willimantic 06226; (860) 456-8548; swiftwaters.org. Open Tues through Fri, noon to 5 p.m.; Sat, 10 a.m. to 5 p.m.; Sun, noon to 4 p.m. Member-owned cooperative of producers—pottery, jewelry, clothing, prints, fine art, photography.

Wadsworth Atheneum Museum Gift Shop, 600 Main St., Hartford 06103; (860) 838-4052; wadsworthshop.org. Open Wed through Fri, 11 a.m. to 5 p.m.; Sat and Sun, 10 a.m. to 5 p.m.; First Thurs, 11 a.m. to 8 p.m. Supports local artists by selling many made-in-Connecticut items.

Appendix C:
More Resources to Find and Buy Connecticut-Made Products

Connecticut Office of Tourism

Ctvisit.com has a list of holiday fairs, farmers' markets, craft shows, etc. where visitors to the state can buy Connecticut-made products. They also have links to the various Connecticut Tourist Trails for visiting producers of wine, cheese, beer, chocolate, and other Connecticut-made food and drink products.

Connecticut Specialty Food Companies

Here's a link to some of the specialty food companies operating in Connecticut. Most encourage visitors, but the link will lead to information about where you can buy these products online, in local stores and chains, or through other distributors: ct.gov/doag/lib/doag/marketing_files/company_list_013012.pdf.

Craft Fairs

A list of these fairs staged all over the state—many held annually and lots of them held during the holiday season or during the warm months outside or in tents can be found online at fairsandfestivals.net.

Farmers' Markets

Held all over Connecticut from late spring to autumn, most feature locally made crafts, small batch food items, local wine, and fresh local produce. Coventry Regional Farmers' Market is an excellent example, as is the market at Nathan Hale

Homestead (2299 South St., Coventry 06238; coventryfarmersmarket.com). A list of most of the markets can be found using this link: ctvisit.com/special-interest-trails/farmers-market-trail/summary/4012.

Open Studios

These events are held all over the state, many in November and December for holiday gift buying or during the summer months. The City of Hartford, and the Quiet Corner (the northeast part of Connecticut) have annual open studio shows. Use a search agent to find those located in other Connecticut towns and cities and for dates and times. Here are a few links: Artists' Open Studios of Northeast CT, aosct .org; Loft Artists Association, loftartists.com; Shoreline Arts Trail, shorelineartstrail .com.

Websites and Other Links

Check out these websites and search for products sold there by Connecticut businesses: Etsy, Facebook, artisansmarketplacect.com.

Index

About the Author

Born and educated in Connecticut, Cynthia Parzych is a writer, book publisher, editor, and professional chef. She lives in Glastonbury, Connecticut, in The Old Parsonage, built in 1693, where she runs her publishing company and a food business using the produce grown on her property and sourced locally to make sauces, soups, pesto, pickles, vinegars, jams, and marmalades all sold from her house and farm stand under The Old Parsonage label.